To Pa...
...

How to learn
- Spanish - French -
German - Arabic -
any foreign language
successfully.

Essential techniques, memory methods, clever ideas and secrets for achieving fluency with foreign languages.

By: Peter Oakfield

Riverbridge Books

This edition published in the United Kingdom by

Riverbridge Books.

192 Leckhampton Road, Cheltenham GL53 0AE   U.K.

ISBN 978-0-9574932-0-9

Copyright © Peter Oakfield 2012

Peter Oakfield has asserted his moral right to be identified as the author of this book.

All rights reserved. No part of this book may be reproduced or utilized in any form or by any means electronic, mechanical or photocopying, or stored in any database or retrieval system.

About the author:

Peter Oakfield lives in the west of England and writes about memory and language learning topics. His other books include *How to transform your Memory and Brain Power: a complete course for memory development, fast learning skills and speed-reading.*

TABLE OF CONTENTS

FOREWORD. ....Page 9

INTRODUCTION. ....Page 11

CHAPTER 1. PREPARING TO LEARN A FOREIGN LANGUAGE. ....Page 13

1.1 Essentials to be considered before starting to learn a foreign language.

1.2 Language Groups: What you need to know.

1.3 Twenty-five Languages: Details of 25 of the most widely spoken languages.

1.4 Learning a foreign language on your own.

1.5 How to maintain your motivation to learn the foreign language.

1.6 Why you need realistic learning targets for the foreign language, and what they should be.

1.7 The diversity approach to foreign language learning: A better way to study.

1.8 Systematic foreign language learning or learning based on situations and language usage. Which is best?

CHAPTER 2. ESSENTIALS AND MATERIALS. ....Page 21

2.1 A checklist of essential materials for foreign language learning.

2.2 How to select the right audio language course.

2.3 What to look for with a computer-program foreign language course.

2.4 How to prepare and use a vital key-plan for foreign language learning.

2.5 How often do you need to study the foreign language to be successful? Follow this plan for more productive studying of your target language.

2.6 The right circumstances for the most effective foreign language learning.

2.7 How to undertake a foreign language study overview: and why it is important to do so.

3

2.8 How much foreign vocabulary do you need to learn?

2.9 A cheap but useful language learning aid.

CHAPTER 3. BASIC APPROACHES TO FOREIGN LANGUAGE LEARNING..**Page 30**

3.1 Where and how best to start the foreign language study.

3.2 How to use a foreign language audio course effectively.

3.3 How to start speaking the foreign language as soon as you start learning it.

3.4 How to put grammar in its place.

3.5 How to achieve correct pronunciation of the foreign language.

3.6 Fast feedback and how to use it for more satisfactory foreign language learning.

3.7 Repetition and recitation techniques for foreign language learning: Why they differ, and how best to use each of them.

3.8 Moving from passive study to dynamic foreign language learning.

3.9 How best to use writing as an aid to foreign language learning.

CHAPTER 4. VALUABLE TECHNIQUES FOR FOREIGN LANGUAGES..**Page 41**

4.1 The visualization technique and how to use it for foreign language learning.

4.2 Speaking aloud: How to make better use of this aid to foreign language learning.

4.3 Note book use for foreign language study.

4.4 Learning idioms and expressions in a foreign language.

4.5 The method of double translation and how to use it to aid learning of the target language

4.6 The Parallel Method and how to use it properly.

CHAPTER 5. A BETTER UNDERSTANDING OF THE FOREIGN LANGUAGE. **Page49**

5.1 The difference between Literal and Literary English translations: Knowing which to use and when.

5.2 A mechanical foreign language fallacy and how to avoid it.

5.3 How to use curiosity to enhance foreign language learning.

5.4 How to develop deeper and better concentration for foreign language study.

CHAPTER 6. MEMORIZING VOCABULARY SUCCESSFULLY..Page 57

6.1 Memorizing vocabulary: How to prepare.

6.2 How to memorize vocabulary: A basic method.

6.3 How to memorize vocabulary: Using simple connections.

6.4 How to memorize vocabulary: The Memory Link Method.

6.5 How to memorize vocabulary: The Group Method.

CHAPTER 7. THE SECRETS OF THE MULTI-LINGUISTS.

....Page 66

7.1 How Queen Elizabeth 1st learned to speak five foreign languages fluently.

7.2 George Borrow: How this remarkable multi-linguist became fluent in numerous languages.

7.3 Charlotte Bronte's foreign language learning methods.

7.4 Roger Ascham and The Scholemaster: The methods of an inspired teacher of foreign languages.

7.5 The amazing multi-linguist Cardinal.

7.6 The secrets of the multi-linguists.

7.7 How anyone with determination can become a multi-linguist.

CHAPTER 8. GAINING CONFIDENCE AND SKILLS WITH THE FOREIGN LANGUAGE ....Page 85

8.1 The use and benefits of analogous application in learning a foreign language

8.2 Staying with a family: how to gain the most from the experience.

8.3 Practicing with native speakers of the foreign language.

8.4 How to improve conversational skills in the foreign language.

8.5 Courses at colleges and with tutors: What you need to consider.

8.6 Whether to have a study-friend.

8.7 How to learn essential grammar easily.

CHAPTER 9. PROGRESSING FURTHER WITH THE FOREIGN LANGUAGE. ....Page 94

9.1 Is it possible for an adult to learn to speak a foreign language the way a child learns to speak?

9.2 How to find time for additional practice.

9.3 How to acquire greater fluency.

9.4 How to overcome apparent difficulties.

9.5 How to deal with challenging foreign language texts.

9.6 Use of formal and informal modes of address in the foreign language.

9.7 The best sources of foreign vocabulary.

9.8 Beware of false friends in foreign language vocabulary.

9.9 Good sources of additional reading material for improving your foreign language skills.

9.10 Some quick tips for easy learning.

CHAPTER 10. ADVANCED FOREIGN LANGUAGE LEARNING TECHNIQUES AND AIDS. ....Page 103

10.1 How to become fluent with numbers in the foreign language.

10.2 Tips for remembering vocabulary gender.

10.3 Making your own foreign language audio recordings.

10.4 The principle of over-learning for foreign languages and how to apply it.

10.5 How to learn to think in the foreign language.

10.6 Use this little-known but very effective technique to achieve a substantial boost to your command of the foreign language.

10.7 Why offensive language should never be used.

10.8 Finding opportunities to speak the foreign language.

10.9 How to cope with fast speech in the foreign language.

10.10 Inaccuracies in foreign language conversation.

CHAPTER 11. AIMING AT COMPLETE MASTERY OF THE FOREIGN LANGUAGE. ....**Page 112**

11.1 How to use interest in the culture as an aid for foreign language learning.

11.2 How to assist your progress with greater enjoyment from the study and use of the foreign language.

11.3 Learning verbs and their conjugations: How to make the task easier.

11.4 Some easily available additional learning resources for the foreign language.

11.5 Use this alternative dictionary to develop deeper learning of the foreign language.

11.6 How to improve self-confidence as an aid to learning the foreign language.

11.7 The importance of rewards.

11.8 How to cope with (and prevent) flagging interest in the foreign language study.

11.9 Why and how regular self-assessments of progress in the foreign language should be made.

11.10 Learning the target language in the language itself.

CHAPTER 12. MAKING SURE OF YOUR SUCCESS WITH THE CHOSEN FOREIGN LANGUAGE. ....**Page 121**

12.1 How to revise the foreign language effectively.

12.2 Alternative foreign language revision methods.

12.3 The lazy man's way to learn a foreign language.

12.4 How to avoid letting the foreign language skills fade away.

12.5 Putting it all together and the global approach.

12.6 A short list of useful terms.

12.7 The important first step.

FOREWORD

Learning a foreign language can be a difficult experience if it is not approached in the right way. Time and attention to the task are needed and it is important that the efforts should result presently in the ability to speak the language. Also the study should progress with reasonable speed. The student needs to be able to put the language to use sooner rather than later because otherwise there may be disenchantment or boredom, resulting in an abandonment of the work.

This book has been written to satisfy these requirements by providing numerous ideas, valuable learning techniques, memory methods and help for acquiring a foreign language, so that any student can be sure of success.

Described here are techniques that are frequently used to achieve foreign language fluency. In addition many other methods are revealed that are novel or not at all well known, but which are highly effective. Equally important is the fact that the techniques described are applicable to the learning of any language.

By following the guidance in this book any anyone wanting to learn a foreign language will discover that they have the ability to do so just as well as anyone else; that no special 'gift for languages' is needed to do so; and that it can be learned it a great deal more quickly than previously might have been imagined possible.

This is a book to keep ready to hand, to read before the study commences and for regular reference as it progresses. It will be an invaluable friend guiding the way to foreign language fluency and showing that the process of learning the language can also be an enjoyable experience.

Here are just a few of the many things you will discover:

How to select the right language learning materials

Dozens of methods and techniques for speedy learning of foreign languages

How to start speaking the foreign language as soon as you start learning it

Several different ways to memorize vocabulary easily and successfully

How to put grammar in its place

Secrets of famous successful multi-linguists that you can use

How to make learning a foreign language really enjoyable

How to improve conversational skills in the foreign language

How to concentrate effectively for foreign language learning

How to learn to think in the foreign language

How to make your foreign language learning successful and fast

The lazy man's way to learn a foreign language

And much more. In total more than 80 important topics for learning a foreign language successfully and quickly are covered.

INTRODUCTION

It's good to be able to speak a foreign and language and better still to be able to speak several. It's fun, it improves the intellect, it's useful, it gives self-assurance, and it can bring rewards such as a better salary, advantages in business, new friends and more interesting employment. Travel in particular is infinitely more enjoyable when the language of the country visited can be spoken. In short, learning a foreign language will open numerous doors that would otherwise have remained closed.

With all these advantages it is unfortunate that so many people despite having 'studied' a foreign language for years at school, cannot speak a word of it, and respond with blank looks to even the simplest expressions in the language studied at school, from those who do speak it.

In fact it is easier than may be realized to learn foreign languages, if it is done the right way. Some people are able to speak numerous foreign languages and there are those who have been outstandingly successful. For example, the writer and traveller George Borrow could speak around thirty languages; and the famous Cardinal Mezzofanti could speak over forty languages fluently and many others to a good standard. In total he could speak around one hundred. More modestly Queen Elizabeth 1st could speak five.

Doubtless some of those who speak a great number of languages may have a natural gift, but equally it is evident that others have employed more efficient learning and memorizing methods and have developed the skills to learn languages, or discovered one or more of them, perhaps by chance. In the course of this book the methods of some of these successful multi-linguists will also be examined, together with numerous other ideas for progressing with the learning of a foreign language.

Because what is important for success in learning a foreign language, is knowing the methods and best approaches and applying them to the study. It is not necessary to have been born with some special ability with languages. As to this it should be remembered that in many countries it is normal for people to be at least bilingual. Such persons do not possess some special capacity, or mental advantage, for speaking more than one language, that those in other countries inexplicably lack. The fact is, that no one is incapable of learning a foreign language if they know how to set about it and are willing to try.

This book is designed to help anyone to learn foreign languages quickly and successfully by providing many different learning approaches, ideas and techniques and explaining how to develop the right mindset to absorb the target language. Study procedures and little known learning and memorizing techniques are included. Those who read this book will have no excuse for not learning a foreign language, because the methods and techniques needed are set out here.

All are explained clearly and to the point. Those who are anxious to know how to learn a foreign language, will find guidance that is concise, understandable and to the point. Then, as the right ways to approach a foreign language are applied it will be seen how effectively they work.

It will also be seen that many of the old teaching methods that may have been a deterrent in the past such as unproductive repetition, undue emphasis on grammar at an early stage, illogical demands (e.g. "you have to learn Latin first"!!) can be forgotten; and that the ability to learn a foreign language and probably 2 or 3 can be enjoyed by anyone.

Of course the necessary time to study will still have to be made available, because what is provided is not a magic language pill. What will be found are the keys to very profitable language learning that will ensure that your efforts really do result in fluency in the target language and that they do so much more swiftly than would otherwise be possible.

CHAPTER 1.

PREPARING TO LEARN A FOREIGN LANGUAGE

1.1 What to consider before starting to learn a foreign language.

Is there any choice as to the foreign language that to be learned? Perhaps a decision has already been made as to what language is to be learned and if so this question may seem inappropriate. Maybe there is no choice. Business or employment, or the demands of education may dictate that a particular language must be learned.

But where there is a choice, then before any commitment is made to what must be a significant amount of studying, and money spent on learning materials, it is as well to consider first whether the foreign language selected will be the best.

Points to consider:

** The economic, business and employment factors that may affect the choice.

** Whether countries where the language is spoken will be visited frequently.

** The level of difficulty - e.g. complex grammar or novel sounds - that the language presents.

** Whether the language is widely spoken or is a minority language.

** Whether there are good prospects for practicing the language as it is learned and for using it thereafter.

** Whether a language in the same group of languages is already known, or whether in the future another language in the same group may be

13

needed. It is easier to learn another language in the same group than it is to learn a language in a completely different group.

** Whether courses, study materials and native speakers for assistance and practice will be reasonably accessible. Whether it will be possible to find a study friend.

It is best to avoid selecting the language just on impulse, or for undefined reasons. Mastering a foreign language can be immensely rewarding; but it would be frustrating to find, after putting in a good deal of effort, that some other language would have made a better choice.

1.2 Language Groups: what you need to know.

Due to common ancestry, many languages fall conveniently into distinct groups or families. For example most of the languages in European countries are accepted as being members of what is known as the Indo-European family. This is a broad category that can be broken down into further subdivisions or closer family groups. One such family within the Indo-European group is the Teutonic that includes the German, Dutch, English, Norwegian and Swedish languages. Further examples are given below.

The classification of a particular language is not just a matter of academic interest. There is an advantage in knowing where a language fits into the various families, because with this information, a more satisfactory choice can be made as to the language to be learned.

Any language that is in the same group as one's mother tongue will obviously be easier to learn, because of the similarities that may occur between the language known and the language to be learned. For the same reason a language in the same group as a language previously mastered, may be a better candidate for future study, than one that is outside the group.

These are the major language groups: -

** Teutonic: German, Dutch, Icelandic, English, Danish, Swedish, Norwegian

** English is in the Teutonic group although it has many Latin based words as a result of its Norman history. Moreover it has shed many of the difficult forms often associated with Teutonic languages.

** Latin/Romance: French, Spanish, Portuguese, Italian, Romanian, Catalan.

** Slavic: Russian, Polish, Bulgarian, Slovakian, Czech, Serbo-Croat, Slovene, Bulgarian, Ukrainian

** Baltic: Lithuanian, Latvian

** Celtic: Erse, Gaelic, Welsh, Breton, Cornish

** Finno-Ugrian: Finnish, Magyar, Estonian, Lappish

** Indic: Hindi, Urdu, Bengali, Punjabi, Sinhalese, Oriya

** Indo-Chinese: Chinese, Tibetan, Thai, Burmese

** Altaic: Turkish, Uzbek, Mongolian, Korean, Japanese

** Afro-Asiatic: Arabic, Hebrew

** Niger-Congo; Swahili, Shona, Xhosa, Zulu

** Malayo-Polynesian: Malay, Indonesian, Maori, Hawaiian

** Caucasian: Georgian, Chechen

1.3 Twenty-Five Languages: Details of 25 of the most widely spoken languages

The exact number of people who speak any language must inevitably be a matter of estimate, but the following is a guide to some of the languages that have great numbers of speakers.

Languages and approximate number of speakers: -

Arabic 270000000

Bengali 215000000

Cantonese 66000000

Chinese Mandarin 1130000000

Chinese Min Nan 48000000

English 500000000

French 195000000

German 100000000

Gujarati 43000000

Hindu/Urdu 470000000

Italian 65000000

Japanese 130000000

Korean 69000000

Malay/Indonesian 165000000

Marathi 65000000

Persian 38000000

Polish 46000000

Portuguese 197000000

Russian 280000000

Spanish 415000000

Tamil 63000000

Telugu 65000000

Turkish 78000000

Ukrainian 41000000

Vietnamese 65000000

1.4 Learning a foreign language on your own.

There are advantages to studying with others but whether or not a foreign language class is attended, and however good any class teaching may be, if a foreign language is to be learned, it will require time to be spent working alone. Being willing to study independently, and to make the necessary time for this available, is important. Moreover whilst being in a class may be helpful, others in the same group may learn more slowly, and if just the class is relied upon it will delay progress. This all means accepting the necessity of regular self-motivated study.

1.5 How to maintain your motivation to learn the foreign language.

Learning a foreign language requires self-discipline as well as encouragement to keep going and these can best be maintained if there is good underlying motivation. One of the ways in which motivation can be fostered is by having a list of the objectives and aspirations for the proposed language study. The reasons for wanting to learn the language and the benefits it will bring need to be thought about carefully. They should then be written down. "I want to learn ------language because------- " This will be the motivation list.

Examples:

** A formal qualification in the language is needed

** Ability to speak the language is required so as to advance in employment or for business advantage.

** A visit to family who live where the language is spoken is anticipated.

** There is an interest in culture associated with the language.

** There are friends who speak the language.

** Travel, work or live where the language is spoken is anticipated.

**Reading the literature of the language is an ambition.

** Educational requirements.

Writing down the reasons identified is important. This is not an unnecessary exercise, which may as well be omitted, but a valuable aid to maintaining the resolution to learn the language. The list prepared should be added to from time to time if further reasons or benefits are thought of; and periodically the list should be read over as a reminder of what will be gained by learning the language. This will revitalize the determination to keep going. Also during the unavoidable times when there is a difficult patch, the list will be a spur to keep the study of the language on track.

17

1.6 Why you need realistic learning targets for the foreign language, and what they should be.

The learning of a foreign language may conveniently be divided into various stages:

** Beginner to Intermediate: By the time this stage is completed it should be possible to read straightforward texts, student readers and children's books; to use the language for holidays and travel; and to conduct conversations that are not complex. The use of the language will be rewarding despite limitations.

** Intermediate to Advanced: On conclusion of this stage the student should be comfortable with more difficult texts, be able to read most books and newspapers, and understand a large part of what is heard on the radio. There will be confidence with the language and an ability to hold more complex conversations.

** Advanced: Little or no difficulty with conversations or texts (other than technical works) should be experienced and the student will be comfortable in nearly all situations. Substantial fluency will be enjoyed and the use of the language will be more or less second nature.

** Fluent: All the ability and fluency of an educated native speaker of the foreign language has been achieved.

It is important to be realistic in deciding what is the correct stage to aim at having regard to the present level of ability. That way success in completing it and enjoying the rewards that it brings is more likely. The ability will have been proven and this will be an incentive to continue the studies towards the next stage up.

1.7 The diversity approach to foreign language learning: a better way to study.

A typical scenario for those learning a foreign language is to buy a textbook and work away at the first few chapters and then to find that a degree of boredom has set in, or that some matter has not been properly understood because of an inadequate explanation in the book. The book perhaps offers limited scope for practicing what has been learned, or may not cover the subject as well as it might, or may on closer acquaintance be found to be unimaginative. There may be too few foreign language examples and exercises or too much grammar or vice versa.

For these reasons, both with textbooks and audio, it is very advantageous to follow more than one course in the target language at the same time. This may sound as though some extra and unnecessary work is to be added to the business of learning the target language, but this should not be the case. If the ancillary materials are used appropriately, it will be found that because they improve the quality of the study and make it more interesting, learning will be better and faster.

Suggestions:

** Studying at least two course books at the same level. One book could be the main source for the study; and the other could be used to provide an alternative view. At least one should include a good explanation of the grammar.

** Following at least two, and perhaps more, audio courses at about the same level. A good arrangement is to have one main high-quality audio course and one or two shorter ones, used for additional experience and practice. There are many cheap audio courses in the main languages and finding them should not be difficult.

The additional courses or books reinforce what is learned with the main course and so will not take so long to work through. Also the different approaches in each course will aid understanding especially of any difficult points. Interest and consequently concentration will be maintained by the variety and the different presentations in each of the courses and by the habit of cross-referencing from one to another. Further exercise opportunities and greater facility to practice what has already been learned will be provided.

The diversity approach is a good method to adopt when learning a foreign language, stimulating greater retention of the material covered, and encouraging a move ahead more satisfactorily. It will be helpful even if the additional textbooks and audio are not followed strictly, but are just dipped into from time to time.

1.8 Systematic foreign language learning or learning based on situations and language usage. Which is best?

The approach to foreign language learning based on introducing the grammar and with a systematic advance through the important stages needed to grasp the language, has now somewhat fallen out of favour.

The method that is most popular currently, is to present the student with typical everyday situations and to encourage the student to develop a command of the language more by usage than by reference to it's structure. The student is intended to learn by repetition and experience of a range of probable everyday scenarios, and not by reference to elements that make up the language. For example the student will learn how to ask the way, how to make a purchase at a shop, how to order a meal at a restaurant, how to talk about their family, etc. Grammar relating to the language will usually be introduced incidentally and in a limited way.

With the grammatical systematic approach, some essential principle will be introduced at each stage, before ways in which it might or should be applied are dealt with. The object is to ensure that the student has a proper grasp of the structure of the language and to apply it accordingly. Exercises are provided that follow and require an understanding and application of the elements of the language that have been introduced.

In reality there is a good deal of overlap between the two methods, so neither could be regarded as excluding the other. Moreover the answer to the question, which is best, is that there is great value in both and that neither should be ignored by any student who wishes to make good progress. Reference should naturally be made to the students own inclinations and preferred learning style, but ideally materials that will provide exposure to both methods of learning should be acquired and studied as part of the diversity approach described above,

See also ahead: **How to put Grammar in its place.**

CHAPTER 2.

ESSENTIALS AND MATERIALS.

2.1 A checklist of essential materials for foreign language learning.

It is much easier to learn a foreign language if there are good materials to show the way, than if there are inadequate resources.

This is a list of essential items:

** A textbook suitable for all fundamental learning stages. It is important that it should contain adequate grammar set out systematically. Even though initially the student may hope not to have to learn the grammar or to study it regularly, it is important to be able to find quickly what is needed, whenever necessary.

** Dictionaries: Ideally three should be acquired. The first should be should be small size so that it can be taken when travelling etc. The second should be a good medium size dictionary; this will be a main working dictionary. The third dictionary should be a more substantial reference dictionary. Nothing like all the vocabulary that it contains will be needed, but without a reference dictionary, it is easy to be stuck when infrequently used words are encountered.

** Notebooks: Several notebooks for summaries, vocabulary and so on are desirable. These should be small enough to put into the pocket for use whenever there are a few spare moments for impromptu revision.

** One or two phrase books. These are a good source of helpful phrases and expressions and useful to have for occasional browsing.

** CD, MP3 or similar audio-player (with a pause control and preferably portable)

** Blank cards (postcard size) to use as flash cards.

** Audio materials: audio courses and recorded dialogues etc.

** TV with DVD player: to watch films in the target language.

** A reference book for verbs and their conjugations in the target language.

Obtaining the right materials for the proposed language study will require some little investment, but the money will be well spent when it is weighed against the benefits that the successful study will bring. By way of comparison consider what might be spent on other interests, entertainments or hobbies, or just the occasional night out, over the period of a few months. Compared to these the expenditure on language study materials will probably be modest.

2.2 How to select the right audio language course.

Audio courses in foreign languages suitable for different levels of ability (for convenience, referred to in this book as 'audio') are widely available and are invaluable in the study of any language. It should be a priority to obtain one at the outset. However there may be too much choice. Which should be selected?

Here are some guidelines:

** Audio with a full transcript in the foreign language is most important. If the transcript also has an English translation it will be still better, but a foreign transcript is essential so that the exact words spoken can be read, leaving no doubt as to what has been heard.

** There should not be much English spoken. Apart from mentioning the track number why should there be any? Does the English serve any function on the audio that could not have been dealt with in some other way? Instructions etc. in English can be given on the transcript or in ancillary notes.

** Likewise there should not at any stage be much introductory music or similar padding. This, like unnecessary English on the audio, is of no benefit whatever to the student and simply uses up the space that should have been used for the spoken foreign language. Also time is wasted listening to the music whilst waiting for the important spoken foreign language to begin.

There is of course a solution to the superfluous music and English on foreign language discs. Transfer the audio to a computer and use a sound editing software program to strip out the unwanted material. Then save the amended audio recordings to an audio-player. Although this task may be time consuming it is worth doing it for benefit of the improved recordings that will be obtained.

** It is useful to have drills and practice sessions. It is very stimulating to hear a question and then be put on the spot by having to answer in the target language. In this way what has been learned has to be utilized quickly; and one can come as close as it is possible, with audio, to experiencing what live conversation would be like.

** Lengthy pauses, during which responses are to be given, just use up space and are unnecessary. Pauses in practice sessions need only be brief because that will encourage a faster response, and if more time is needed the pause control on the audio player can be used.

** Audio with a story line may help to maintain interest and attention; but typical every day situations are important also.

** Audio should not have excessive repetition of the same phrases etc. Repetition is not necessary because the rewind or track controls on the audio player can be used to go over the same material as often as need be.

** A good audio will provide plentiful vocabulary expressions and idioms. Ask the supplier for details of the amount of vocabulary introduced in the course.

** The foreign language on the audio should be spoken only by native speakers. This will probably be the case but again check this with the supplier.

** The audio should preferably have a number of different speakers, so as to provide experience with a good range of voices. This is better than having just the same two or three people speaking. Once again check this out with the supplier before purchasing.

**The inclusion of cultural background relating to the foreign language would be an added advantage and make the course more interesting.

** Before making a purchase decision that will involve any significant expenditure, see if a sample lesson can be obtained to try out, and check whether the supplier has a 'money back if not satisfied policy'.

If any audio considered is not perfect but is not expensive, it may be worth buying anyway; but buy something more satisfactory as well.

2.3 What to look for with a computer-program foreign language course.

It is important to be sure that any computer program course for learning a foreign language program, that might be bought, will provide a good means of helping you to learn.

To learn a foreign language it is necessary to read it, to hear it, to understand it, to write it, to speak it, to practice it, and to engage the memory with it, so that it becomes second nature and so that it can be spoken without having to think about it. The computer program should assist the achievement of most of these things, as should any type of course.

What is not wanted is a program that does not properly stimulate learning, or that requires undue amounts of time to be spent loading, preparing, and then clicking from place to place, with lengthy waits for answers and so on. If it does so, then it may give the impression of being a learning aid, because it will create activity, but may in fact be making poor use of your valuable time.

On the other hand a computer program that generates progress in learning, and/or gives accurate feedback as to the accuracy of the learner's spoken use of the target language will be valuable, especially if no native speaker is available to criticize and correct any faulty pronunciation. And for many people learning on a computer can be very much more effective than the more traditional methods.

Moreover having a variety of methods and resources when learning is always advantageous. So if the price of the course is right, then it will be well worth acquiring as part of your diversity approach to learning the target language

Before purchasing, advantage should be taken of any trial offers, demonstration discs or sample lessons that the manufacturer may be offering. And even if they are not offered why not try asking for sample materials anyway?

24

2.4 How to prepare and use a vital key-plan for foreign language learning.

A key-plan is a reasonable achievement target -- that is, the level of skill at which you are currently aiming in the language: i.e. beginner to intermediate, intermediate to advanced, etc.-- coupled with a realistic time scale within which to reach it; and a program for the study within the time scale.

A key-plan should show the number of weeks of anticipated study needed to achieve the target, and the amount of work or details of the particular lessons and so on, to be allocated to each week. The plan should be kept handy and each day or each week ticked off as the work is completed. The existence of the plan provides a prompt to study and a reminder to put in more time if the time scale is allowed to slip. It is a useful aid to self-discipline; and helps prevent any pretence that studying has gone on, when the language study has in fact been neglected.

2.5 How often do you need to study the foreign language to be successful? Follow this study plan for more productive learning of your target language.

In order to learn a foreign language it is preferable to study for some period every single day. It is by means of regular daily study that the key plan will be completed, and success with the language achieved, much more so than by occasional study, or with study on just one or two days per week. For example 30 minutes study every day (total 3.5 hours by the end of the week) is far more valuable than studying for 3.5 hours all on one day, once a week (in the unlikely event that there really was a single 3.5 hour session devoted to the study every week without fail).

With daily study there is greater recall of previous work in every session, giving each occasion of study a stronger base on which to build. On the other hand, if the work is neglected, for say a week, it will be found that a good deal more revision is needed to get back up to the level of the last study, before the new material can satisfactorily be tackled.

Also a long study session becomes less effective as it progresses. Tiredness inevitably sets in before the session has ended and

25

concentration begins to wane. Generally any study session should be limited to between 30 minutes and one hour, after which a break should always be taken, before any study is resumed.

Another reason for studying daily is that when any session is ended, the material covered will tend to run on in the mind for a while, even though one is then occupied with other matters. This can amount to a considerable additional bonus of effortless impression on the memory following each study session. Obviously those who study daily will get six times more of this advantage than those who study just once a week.

Also it is better to have 2 separate study sessions per day if that is possible; for example, 20 or 30 minutes in the morning and another 20 or 30 minutes in the evening. The period divided in this way will give greater benefit due to the better recollection and run on effect as described above. If the second session cannot be so lengthy, then perhaps a few minutes later in the day could be found to go over once more what was studied earlier. And when for any reason there has not been time for fresh study on a particular day, then it would be advantageous to take at least ten minutes last thing at night on that day, to revise the last lesson that was studied.

2.6 The right circumstances for the most effective learning.

Having the right background circumstances for studying, namely peace, quiet, comfort, and freedom from distractions, is conducive to more satisfactory results and to a better and more enjoyable learning curve.

For example:

** The Place: The ideal place to study is quiet secluded room, where work can be carried out without other people being present. Best of all is a room used regularly for the purpose because the habit of concentration is helped in familiar surroundings that are associated with steady mental work. On entering a room used principally for study, the mind will more naturally begin to deliver the required concentration.

** Distractions such as television, newspapers and telephones should be banished from the study room. And it is a good idea to pin up the motivation list and the key plan, so that the important objectives are always in view.

** The study materials should be on the desk, ready to hand so that there is no need to prepare them or to start looking for them when the room is entered for the study session. This again is a simple way of ensuring that the mind is comfortable and ready for learning at each appointed time; and not given any opportunity for procrastination.

** It is best not to have others present when studying because of the need for peace and quiet and so as to be able to speak aloud the foreign language as the study progresses. If others are around then inevitably this cannot be done so satisfactorily.

** The absence of noise is an important factor. If people can be heard chattering, or if there are household noises, the work will not be so good. Nor should any music, whether just background or otherwise, be played. If there is music then part of the mind will unavoidably be given to hearing it, and concentration will suffer. A further reason for keeping the study area free from noise is to permit the language audio to be played and then for the student to speak aloud whilst practicing the language, and to hear and assess the result accurately.

** Position: The right position for studying is one in which the student is neither relaxed nor uncomfortable, but is comfortable whilst being gently alert. A sitting posture should be adopted but preferably not in an armchair or sofa where relaxation may cause inattention. A desk or table for books and audio is essential.

2.7 How to undertake a foreign language study overview, and why it is important to do so.

A good exercise before any detailed study of the target language begins, is to undertake an overview of the entire subject; in other words to have an outline picture of what the whole study will entail from beginning to end. Knowing the subject in outline makes learning the detail easier, because there is a mental view of where, how, and why the study is leading, how far there is to go, where each part fits into the whole, and what ground is going to be covered etc.

With these advantages the mind comes better prepared for the substantive study; understanding and concentration are enhanced; and the work generally will progress more comfortably. Carrying out an overview is not a lengthy task and the benefits gained will always reward the effort of doing it, as will be realized when the detailed study is started.

Overview Methods: -

** Reading the introduction in the language textbooks and audio courses.

** Reading the table of contents, the chapter headings and the descriptions of chapters.

** Reading quickly through the introductory paragraphs in each chapter, followed by the foreign text examples and exercises in each chapter or lesson.

** Skim reading the English language examples in each chapter or lesson, and the English parts of the exercises and the English answers.

** Skim reading the whole text 2 or 3 times, paying particular attention to headings and subheadings.

** Making a diagram of the main points and matters, situations, tenses, adjectives, numbers, gender etc. to be covered in the key plan.

** As the language study progresses, repeating the overview from time to time so as to reinforce it.

2.8 How much foreign vocabulary do you need to learn?

If your English/foreign language dictionary contains 150,000 or more translations and even the pocket dictionary seems endless, the mere thought of learning enough foreign vocabulary may be disheartening. It will be reassuring to know that in fact far less vocabulary is needed than might be imagined.

A practical assessment is as follows: -

** Simple communications - e.g. food, drink, accommodation, asking directions, polite exchanges: - a few hundred words will suffice to be understood.

** Most schoolchildren use a vocabulary of scarcely 1000 words and most people should be able to get around reasonably when they have learned this amount.

28

** 2000 to 3000 words will give a good level of vocabulary for conversations and reading at a more detailed level

** 3000 to 4000 words will give comfortable ability in most conversations and in reading more challenging texts.

2.9 A cheap but useful language learning aid.

Flash cards are one of the cheapest, and easiest aids to use when learning a foreign language. The idea is simple: words, phrases, and other material to be learned are written in the foreign language on one side of the cards and the English equivalent is written on the other. Each card is taken in turn, both sides are read, and then each line is read on either the English or the foreign side whilst trying to recollect and repeat the translation on the other. The card is turned over to check accuracy before a further attempt is made.

The cards will have to be written out, which is a little time consuming, but the act of thinking about the words, and then writing them down is a further aid to concentration and memory. Especial care should be taken when writing out the foreign language side of the card, to make sure that there are no errors that are later assumed to be correct and relied upon.

Another use for the cards is for learning verb conjugations, with each card being used to set out all the conjugations for one different verb.

Blank cards are readily available from stationers where they are sold with printed lines as file cards, and are the approximate size of postcards. This convenient size is ideal because a pack of them can be carried around easily for practice whenever there are spare moments. Making use of snippets of time to study the target language is a good way to keep the subject in mind and to maintain your progress.

The cards that have been learned thoroughly can be put on one side, but kept available for periodic revision, and new ones inserted in the pack as often as necessary.

Flash cards are cheap and cheerful and their flexibility and the fact that they can be taken anywhere, for impromptu study as suggested, particularly increases their effectiveness.

CHAPTER 3.

BASIC APPROACHES TO FOREIGN LANGUAGE LEARNING.

3.1 Where and how best to start the foreign language study.

Textbooks, dictionaries and one or more audio courses have been acquired. How should the work begin?

It is best to start with the audio course because with it the foreign language can be listened to and pronounced correctly from the outset. Anyone who begins with a textbook and starts learning vocabulary without audio, in other words without having heard the correct sounds, would be likely to develop incorrect pronunciation, and this can be very difficult to lose once it is acquired. Starting with correct pronunciation makes learning easier, as well as bringing the study of the language properly alive.

The main audio course should be followed for a few lessons, until you are acquainted with the pronunciation and a good number of words, phrases, simple expressions, and short sentences have been learned. Then some of the other learning materials can be introduced and studied in tandem with the main audio. In this way the benefits of a diversity approach to the language will be enjoyed, with each of the different materials reinforcing and adding to what has been learned in the others.

3.2 How to use a foreign language audio course effectively.

An audio foreign language course is an essential tool for the language. The flexibility of use available with the audio material on CD player computer or audio player that can be stopped, rewound, repeated and so on, means that an enormous advantage is now enjoyed in foreign language learning that previous generations had to do without. But it is not enough just to listen to the audio material; it has to be worked at if the most benefit is to be derived from it.

Suggestions: -

** Always have the foreign transcript to hand to refer to as necessary.

** Each portion of audio to be studied should be just a few minutes long (4 or 5 minutes is ideal) so as to be digestible and not overwhelming. Ideally the lessons would provide the audio so that it can be used in this way.

** An English translation of the foreign audio text should be prepared. This can also be used for learning by the parallel method (this is discussed later).

** Listen to the audio whilst reading the foreign transcript. Listen whilst reading your English translation. Listen without reading either. Listen using the pause control and repeat every phrase aloud several times. Leave the audio aside and try to translate the English translation back into the foreign version.

Repeat all these steps several times until the lesson is known really well and confidence and fluency in translating the material either way has been achieved.

** Use a voice recorder to record the reading aloud of the foreign version, compare it with the original and correct any pronunciation errors with repetition.

** Use and repeat regularly the practice sessions on the course.

** Always do all the exercises provided.

3.3 How to start speaking the foreign language as soon as you start learning it.

When learning a foreign language it is not enough just to study the lessons; it is important also to start using the language however little is known at first. This does not mean you should expect to speak with fluency after just a few lessons; but that all that has been learned at any time should be employed straightaway, and not be put aside until the next study session. If a practice is made of starting to use without delay what has been studied, it will be remembered more easily, and the process of speaking and thinking in the language will be prompted, even from the earliest stages of learning.

Suggestions: -

** Creating new sentences from the vocabulary learned; perhaps with just simple substitution of one or two words. For example change the objects mentioned, or the person speaking, or the period they are speaking about----past, present, future etc.

** Talking to oneself in the language using whatever words have been learned.

** Whilst going about daily tasks (even simple matters such as getting up in the morning, cooking, going to work and so on) trying to make up sentences in the language about what is being done. If a complete sentence cannot be constructed, then saying the words for the objects seen, and for the activities undertaken.

** Always doing all the audio practice sessions available on the course; and spending a little time each day both doing a new one and repeating one previously completed.

** Upon meeting someone who speaks the target language then saying something however simple in the language: for example, 'good morning', 'good-bye', 'how are you?' and not being concerned if the reply cannot always be understood.

** Adapting texts from course materials to refer to oneself and friends

** Imagining conversations that might be had with someone else, or trying and translate into the target language conversations actually had during the day.

3.4 How to put grammar in its place.

When learning a foreign language it is necessary to steer between the Scylla of excessive grammar and the Charybdis of none at all. In the past, grammar was sometimes intensively taught as though it alone was the language. On the other hand grammar is sometimes now treated as nonessential and as something that may be passed over hastily or brushed aside. Neither extreme is sensible.

Excessive attention to grammar is obviously not satisfactory. But nor is it helpful to ignore grammar, because despite what may sometimes be suggested to the contrary, it is neither unnecessary nor irrelevant to the study of a foreign language. It is in fact a useful friend that, used correctly, can help to speed up the learning of the target language. What is important is to have the right balance and to avoid either too great an emphasis on grammar, or too little.

Grammar should be looked at in this way: - namely that it is nothing more than an explanation of the ways in which words and syntax change when circumstances change: - e.g. such as the person who is speaking, whether they are speaking as to the past, the future, the present etc. For example we say in English "I drink " but "He drinks" and it would sound odd if anyone were to say, "He drink". These sorts of variations are determined by the grammar of the target language, and the variations need to be known if the language is to be spoken correctly.

An absence of knowledge of the grammar would also mean that the advantage of many short cuts to fluency and understanding in the target language would be missed. Suppose, for example, that the student has learned how to say, "I drink" in the language. If the rules are learned that affect the way in which verb changes for the different persons who might be speaking, then the key is held to being able also to say "you drink, he drinks, we drink, they drink..." Whilst these are nearly all the same in English - although not quite - in foreign languages it may be found that they do not behave so conveniently and that they are frequently all different. The same may be true of adjectives, nouns and other parts of sentences.

When the grammar rules are learned, then a single sentence that has been understood can be adapted so as to fit different circumstances when they occur, and without the need to memorize a different sentence for each such circumstance.

Moreover failure to learn grammar may result in an inability to find the right words or expressions to meet altered circumstances unless the possible individual variations have been laboriously memorized. Of course a student who has not studied the grammar, may perhaps, by dint of lengthy practice, by trial and error and by being corrected by native speakers, work out or guess at some parts of the rules.

And possibly there may be, instinctively, an element of analogous application. All this is a harder way to learn the language than to do so by learning what is generally a more modest amount of grammar than may be thought. Meanwhile a failure to learn grammar will too easily result in misunderstandings and embarrassing mistakes.

Not knowing any grammar for a foreign language might be compared with the difficult job that a child would have in trying to learn to read by the look-and-say method only, and without knowing the sounds for the letters of the alphabet. It may be possible for some to do this but it is hard work, endless mistakes are likely to be made and progress will be slow at best. How much easier it is when the sounds are known. Any written words say can then be worked out and also words can be spelt even though they have never been seen before. Grammar performs a similar function by providing essential scaffolding for the target language.

A further problem for anyone who does not trouble to learn the grammar for the language, is that it can be difficult to discover the meaning of many foreign words even with the aid of a dictionary. The problem lies in the fact that a word may change its spelling and pronunciation, depending upon the grammar of the sentence in which it is used. Whilst the dictionary may give a primary meaning, it will probably not give all the variations that occur when the context, in which the word is used, changes.

For example a verb will usually only be shown in a dictionary as the infinitive. This would be, in English with the word 'to' in front of it. I.E. 'to spin', 'to run'. A foreign language speaker learning English would need to know that the rule for these words gives past tenses of 'span' 'ran' etc. English is relatively easy for most verb tenses; but this may not be the case with many foreign languages. And unless the rules are more or less known, it will be hard to find out the meaning of a word that has changed due to the grammar of the particular language.

So far as textbooks and grammar are concerned, it is best to look at several before deciding which to buy. What is needed is a book that sets the grammar out in regular form and systematically, so that the way around it can be found easily; and referred back to swiftly for particular points when necessary. Also it should have a pleasant style, good explanations, and ample examples. It should concentrate on the essentials and it should not distract with forms that are only rarely going to be met in practical usage, if at all.

If the right textbook is acquired, it will soon demonstrate the value of grammar in the study of the target language and learning it will be neither difficult nor boring. And in the process any lack of knowledge of English grammar (so far as such knowledge may be helpful in the study of the target language) that the student may have had to start with, will be remedied, as any good textbook covering the foreign language grammar will teach all the essentials that are needed.

The terminology of grammar may be a deterrent for some people. If bothered by the mention of words such as 'participle', 'conjugate', 'decline' etc., it will be reassuring to know that the total of such terms necessary is very little. See ahead: '**A short list of useful terms**'. The terms are a form of shorthand to convey the meaning of grammatical forms, without the need to repeat the explanation as to the meaning on each occasion that the particular form is to be discussed. There is no need for the terms to be memorized. The list should just be referred to as necessary and the terms will soon be understood well enough.

3.5 How to achieve correct pronunciation of the foreign language.

Correct pronunciation is an essential part of learning a foreign language. It is important that the language sounds right when it is spoken, and in view of the efforts that will be put into mastering the other essentials, it would be regrettable if the matter of pronunciation were to be neglected. Moreover it is only with satisfactory pronunciation that one can expect to be understood properly; and without it attempts to speak the language may not be understood at all.

With this in mind, it is essential that the mistake of acquiring bad pronunciation should be avoided or the errors will have to be unlearned and that may be difficult to achieve if poor pronunciation has become ingrained. This means not trying to learn pronunciation from those who are not native speakers; and not trying to learn just from textbooks, although reading textbook advice as to the sounds of letters will be helpful, provided that it is used only in addition to learning by listening to, and imitating native speakers.

35

Luckily audio courses prepared with native speakers are readily available and also the help of native speakers might be enlisted to make one's own audio if necessary. Really, audio recordings are about the best way to develop the desired good accent. The recordings can be played again and again, repeating individual phrases and sentences as often as need be. This is even better than periodic tutorials with a native speaker without any audio.

Further suggestions:

** Using the pause control on the audio after every phrase or sentence and repeating it aloud.

** Being careful not to apply English pronunciation to the foreign word, especially when the foreign word looks similar to the English one.

** Listening for the tone and cadence of the language and trying to capture it whilst repeating from the audio.

** Always having a transcript ready to hand when whilst working on the audio so that each word can be checked as to what it may be, but also listening and repeating without it so that full concentration is given to the sound.

** On occasional use of the audio, trying to speak simultaneously with the foreign speaker. This will oblige a greater attention to be paid.

3.6 Fast feedback and how to use it for more satisfactory foreign language learning.

Everyone who has learned a foreign language at school, will have had the experience of undertaking an exercise, submitting it for marking by a teacher and receiving it back a few days or even week or two later with corrections. This is not an efficient or satisfactory arrangement when learning a language. If mistakes are not corrected promptly then the wrong versions will be in the mind until they are corrected, and instead of mentally reinforcing accuracy, errors will have been reinforced and absorbed.

What is needful when learning a foreign language is to have all translations and other work corrected as speedily as possible, ideally at once and certainly not hours or, worse still, days later. The faster the feedback the sooner the right version can understood, digested, and rehearsed mentally.

Here are some ways to achieve fast feedback:

** Using flash cards and checking accuracy as soon as each word or phrase has been spoken.

** Checking translations against any model answers in the textbook immediately after completing an exercise.

** Using the parallel method (see ahead **The Parallel Method** where this is explained) with the audio; and, when translating either way - foreign text to English or vice versa - checking accuracy after each phrase or sentence.

** When using notebooks, always employing the parallel method to set out notes and texts, and translating each way, checking whilst going along.

** When practicing with a native speaker asking to have any errors corrected at once; and then writing down the correct version and repeating it several times.

3.7 Repetition and recitation techniques for foreign language learning: Why they differ, and how best to use each of them.

Repetition and recitation are two important techniques for language learning that often are not properly understood. Follow the guidance below so as to understand and apply them correctly.

REPETITION: As usually engaged in, this amounts to little more than numerous re-readings of the same text. Attempts to learn or to memorize in this way result swiftly in boredom, a lack of concentration, and very little learned in proportion to the effort applied. However repetition for foreign language study can be made productive if applied in the right way.

Suggestions: -

** Repeating any material studied by going over it again quickly, one final time at the end of the study period.

** When revising from notes always ending by a quick skim read of the same pages that have been revised.

** While repeating, thinking constructively about the language and ways in which what is learned can be applied. E.G. By planning answers to exercises and by thinking about situations in which any new vocabulary, idioms and expressions etc. can be put to use

** Making fresh written notes when the same material is studied again, even if the written notes are thrown away afterwards.

** Setting down the material on flash cards and shuffling them so as to achieve a different order when the cards are repeated

** Repeating in discussion study friend, the material that has been studied.

** Making a quick revision of the days study at the end of each day.

** Repeating aloud, important elements of the study and especially any words and particularly phrases to be learned, before starting to memorize them.

RECITATION. Recitation is superficially similar to repetition; but recitation, being essentially repetition by attempting to recall the studied material just from memory, is a dynamic process and therefore much more effective in the creation of a permanent memory path, than simple repetition which is inclined to be passive.

A typical example of recitation would be trying to recall the contents of a page, or even just a few lines of a text that has been covered over after it has been read. The attempted material is then uncovered and any mistakes noted, before a further recall attempt is made with the page again covered over.

Recitation is an important means of learning and imposing material on the memory.

Several suggestions are made for its use: -

** Memorizing vocabulary: covering over either the English or the foreign version and trying to recollect the other.

** After completing a translation of foreign language to English, covering over the foreign version and translating the English back into the foreign version before checking accuracy. If not accurate then doing it again until it is correct each time.

** Using flash cards and not turning them over until a good attempt has been made to try and recall the version on the other side.

** Studying with another person and testing each other on a translation, perhaps line by line.

Recitation is an excellent means of stimulating greater mental involvement with whatever is to be learned because of the challenge that it presents. It requires the portion of foreign language studied to be put into practice, or recalled from memory, without delay. It prompts the correction of any errors, and because the memory has been challenged, it is improved and recollection is easier in future.

3.8 Moving from passive study to dynamic foreign language learning.

During a study period it is easy sometimes to appear to be engaged with the subject matter, but really to be doing little more than just passively looking at or listening to it. The course textbooks may be read and the audio turned on; but this can all too easily become undemanding work with ample opportunity for the mind to slip quietly away from the job even whilst apparently still engaged in reading and listening.

If only such passive work were enough for the language to be learned, but it is not. It is not possible just to listen or read without effort and find with delight that the subject has been mastered. The proof comes at the end of any lesson that has only been received passively, when a test is made of how much can be remembered and it is realized just how little has been absorbed.

Now the lesson must be redone and this time to impose the language forcefully on the memory, a move is needed from a passive to a dynamic study in which concentration is fully maintained and memory is challenged constantly. It is by being challenged, in trying to remember and checking the efforts frequently, both as the lesson progresses and when it has been completed, that a reliable memory of the language will be developed.

A study can further be made dynamic by other challenges and aids to concentration; for example by stopping periodically for questions, reviewing each page mentally before moving to the next, by using recitation etc. In this book various ways to achieve dynamic study are suggested or adapted in various guises as will be seen.

3.9 How best to use writing as an aid to foreign language learning.

Writing is a helpful aid to learning. If what has to remembered is written down it will be easier to recall it afterwards, even though the writing may be thrown away almost at once. The act of writing will have focused the mind, and therefore the memory on the subject, more pointedly than just reading would do. So it is a good idea to write down the essentials of grammar and vocabulary as a preliminary to memorizing them. Writing can also give practice in the active use of the target language.

Other writing suggestions:

** Writing down all translations from English into the foreign language and vice versa.

** Making up and writing down sentences to illustrate points or vocabulary to be remembered.

** Writing letters in the target language to a pen pal. Also writing essays or some descriptive passages in the language.

** Reading a magazine article in the target language, and then putting it away and writing, in the same language, a new version of what was covered. This should not be a repeat of exactly the same words as the original, but the same subject differently expressed in the foreign language.

** Writing out foreign language texts studied. The writing can be thrown away afterwards but the exercise will have reinforced the memory of the text.

** Having studied a point of grammar, writing out an explanation of it (in your own words so as to heighten concentration).

CHAPTER 4.

VALUABLE TECHNIQUES FOR FOREIGN LANGUAGES.

4.1 The visualization technique and how to use it for foreign language learning.

Visualizing or imagining is the making of pictures in the minds eye even though they cannot really be seen, or in reality the object imagined may never have been seen. Perhaps indeed the visualized object could not possibly exist except in the imagination. The ability to do this is a function of the right hand side of the brain, which is considered to be responsible for creativity, the left hand side being responsible for logic and reason.

It is generally accepted that when learning undue emphasis is usually placed on the left hand brain and that the right hand is under-involved. Visualization is a means of encouraging right hand brain involvement and a good increase in memory-power and learning can be achieved by employing it.

Suggestions: -

** When memorizing vocabulary "seeing" the objects as the foreign words are repeated and learned.

** When reading or repeating a foreign phrase or sentence "seeing" the action, the situation and the things involved.

** When working with audio or reading a text, visualizing being present as one of the characters in the piece, and being involved in the dialogue actively. Being one of the persons; being one of the people to whom the others speak; being the person who replies, etc.

** Closing your eyes when visualizing and memorizing. An example of this can be seen with the demonstrations of extraordinary memory powers that are sometimes undertaken by stage performers. An important part of the performers ability is based on visualization processes.

Usually when a particularly difficult feat of memorization has to be undertaken - e.g. memorizing a pack of shuffled cards or numerous items in exact numerical order - the performer will announce that the list of items is only going to be read out to him; he will not be able to see them, because he is going to put on a blindfold.

He will claim that 'this is so as to make it even more difficult'. The truth is the opposite. The blindfold makes the memorization a good deal easier because visualization and the related memorization, is improved with the eyes shut. That is why the performer puts the blindfold on.

This secret can be put to good use. Just close your eyes whilst visualizing as described above. As will be appreciated when this is done, the visualization and the memory of the matter studied are more powerful when the real world is shut out for a few moments so that nothing can be 'seen' but what is imagined.

4.2 Speaking aloud: How to make better use of this aid to foreign language learning.

Speaking aloud is an easy, undemanding technique that will pay a good dividend in foreign language progress; and it should be regular practice for the learner to speak aloud as often as possible, every foreign word phrase and sentence that is used, whether in audio work, reading, memorizing, or just translating.

The advantage of speaking aloud lies in the fact that it requires greater attention and concentration. The involvement of the faculties of both speech and hearing mean that there is greater focus on the material. It is not possible to let the text slip past only partly attended to when reading it aloud. Also speaking aloud means that those new sounds, words and phrases are being practiced. The new sounds are tested on the ear, and can be corrected as necessary.

Lastly fluency is improved by speaking aloud. By being accustomed to expressing the words aloud, they will cease to feel awkward, and instead become natural.

Even when not alone, and so unable comfortably to speak aloud, for example when on a bus or train, it may be possible perhaps, to sub-vocalize whilst reading the studied foreign text and gain much of the benefit of speaking aloud.

4.3 Note book use for foreign language study.

It's good practice to keep a notebook with details of essentials such as points of grammar, vocabulary, and useful extracts from any exercises. Extra interest can be added by inserting cultural points, proverbs, poetry, recipes, etc. in the target language.

Notebook use:

** Can help to reinforce an overview of the subject.

** Encourages better concentration on the subject, as it is prepared.

** Can be used to record essential points for reference and memorizing.

** Is ideal for speedy revision.

** Can be taken in the pocket to study in spare moments. (The value of frequent study - a little and often - cannot be overstated.)

4.4 Learning idioms and expressions in a foreign language.

Every language has a fair share of polite expressions, commonly used sayings and phrases, noncommittal expressions, and idioms, the latter being peculiar modes of expressions that seem sometimes to defy the rules of grammar for the language. Being used to them, one is hardly aware of them in English but when a foreign language is studied they can leap out, irrational, tiresome and with the seeming intention of making the task of learning more difficult.

These types of linguistic forms have to be learned without worrying unduly about the rules of grammar or logic. It is a matter of accepting that, if that's the way it is said, then that is the way it must be learned. Moreover it is most important not to try and avoid, or to delay, learning idiomatic oddities in the language. The language needs to be learned as it is and as it is spoken. It has to be taken as it comes.

The best way to learn idioms and expressions is to be on the look out for them and note them down promptly. However the exact meaning of each of the words involved needs to be found out and written down as well as the practical meanings of the expressions. They should then be transferred to flash cards or note-books and practiced until they have been completely mastered.

4.5 The method of double translation and how to use it to aid learning of the target language.

The method of double translation has similarities with the parallel method, which is described ahead. The idea of double translation is to take a text in the foreign language, to translate it into English, and then, after leaving it on one side for a while, to try to translate it back into the foreign language. When this has been done, the result is checked against the original foreign text to see how satisfactory the translation has been.

Double translation is a very powerful learning technique, and provides an excellent means of approaching and developing the student's understanding and use of the target language.

With double translation the student is always required to begin by preparing his own English version from the foreign text, instead of relying on any ready prepared translation. Moreover double translation, although clearly akin to the parallel method, would not necessarily be used afterwards for the parallel method, but could be just a routine exercise, with a completely different foreign text used each time.

Moreover, unlike the parallel method, double translation does not require that the translation back into the foreign language should have exactly the same words as the original. What is necessary is that the student's attempt to render the text once more into the foreign language should contain all the sense and intended communication of the original and that it should present a good use of the target language.

But the result of the attempt might be achieved with some different foreign language forms, vocabulary and tenses, provided that all are grammatically correct. The student learns not just by undertaking the two translations, but also by the subsequent comparison of his foreign version with the original, and seeing how his attempt to write in the target language could be improved.

The exercise of double translation can be somewhat demanding, but equally it will be found to be one that is very rewarding.

4.6 The Parallel Method and how to use it properly.

The parallel method, which has already been referred to briefly, is the study of a foreign text in the target language with an accurate English translation used alongside as a learning tool. This was formerly called a "crib"- and was often used by schoolboys in Victorian times for the then obligatory learning of Latin and Greek. The method is a valuable aid for the learning of a foreign language.

The English version used should be closely faithful to the foreign text, reasonably literal, and certainly not a literary translation (see ahead - **Literal and Literary English Translations**). Moreover the English should be a translation from the foreign text and not vice versa. This is an important point. The foreign language used has to be the correct foreign form, taken either from an audio transcript, or from text-books or other accurate source, and then translated into English. The object of the English translation in the parallel method is to provide a very accurate prompt back to the foreign language text, and not to provide a text for an independent translation into the foreign language.

With an audio transcript, and with many textbooks, there may, with luck, be a good English translation provided. Additionally, for many languages, there are books of short stories, and other works provided in parallel English and foreign language forms that might be used for this method. But it is important to make sure that whatever source is taken does indeed deliver a reasonably close or literal translation, before it is relied upon; and that efforts to learn words are not wasted because they are later found to mean something different from those that were indicated.

English translations, even those expressly provided for language study purposes, regrettably are not always close or literal and can be unsatisfactory or even quite misleading. This means usually that some work will be needed with a dictionary to make quite sure that the parallel English version is really accurate before it is used.

The parallel method facilitates learning by requiring the student to try and recall the original foreign sentences, and also by encouraging recitation of the text used. Either the English or the foreign text can be covered with a card and as the open version is read, it is then translated line by line, into the other, either speaking it aloud or writing it down, with the card being moved down just enough to check accuracy as progress is made through the text. Once the foreign version is reasonably understood, the student will of course concentrate on reading the English and translating into the foreign version.

Having the right layout is important so as to get the best from the parallel method. One layout is to have the foreign and English versions in two vertical columns each alongside the other, and with each line not containing too much text. With luck there may be enough room on the transcript page provided with the audio course, to be able to rule lines on the transcript next to the foreign version, and then to write in the English alongside to achieve the two parallel columns.

Although double columns on the original audio transcript page are a quick way to achieve parallel versions, this may not always be practical, especially if the foreign text is not conveniently printed with sufficient room left for the English version. Also it is best to avoid writing out the foreign version as well, due to the risk of writing any part of it inaccurately. So where there is not enough space for the double columns on the original page, one solution is to number each of the lines of the foreign text and then write out the English translation on matching numbered lines, set out perhaps at the bottom of the same page or on a separate sheet of paper.

One comfortable form, perhaps the best, with the parallel method, is to have a notebook with the foreign text on one page, and the English translation on the opposite facing page. Each line of foreign text is numbered, with the corresponding English being likewise numbered. Perhaps the foreign version could be cut and pasted into the notebook. A5 is a convenient size and when using this notebook format it would not be necessary to have a card to cover over the opposite foreign or translation version. The notebook can be held with the opposite page turned away a little, so that it does not catch the eye as the other page is read and translated (except when checking).

In whatever way the work is arranged, what is wanted is to have is to have foreign language and English texts instantly referable one to the other, line by line, for easy and swift cross checking of translation accuracy. Ideally they should not be more than a page apart, so that delays in any checking of the translated version against the original are minimized.

The parallel method: -

** Allows immediate correction of translating mistakes - fast feedback.

** Removes any necessity to recheck words in a dictionary if the correct translation is forgotten and avoids the loss of time occasioned by doing so.

**Allows accurate learning with greater ease.

** Helps improve fluency.

** Is the perfect partner for learning by recitation.

** Assists closer acquaintance with the correct foreign language forms. Also attention and practice can more easily be given to speaking the language the way it should be spoken. Additionally it helps the subsequent development of language skills by means of analogous application (discussed ahead).

Victorian schoolmasters used to dismiss a crib as something that only lazy schoolboys would employ. And this curious view has not entirely disappeared. Even today parallel translations are sometimes criticized as "making it too easy", as though the foreign language study ought to be difficult. Such criticisms have lost sight of the reason why the language is being studied. The object is not to have a hard time but to learn to speak the language.

Nonetheless it is important to bear in mind that the parallel method, though extremely valuable, is ultimately only a stepping-stone to help the student to cross the flood from the shore of the English language and to place a foot on the shore of the target language. Presently, when a reasonable command of the new language begins to be developed, the aid that the parallel method provides should be abandoned and the effort made to progress without it.

Otherwise, a continued reliance on the parallel method could result in a translation mindset - that is, always thinking in English and translating mentally to the target language before speaking it. Instead the student ought in due course begin to try to learn the target language substantially in the language itself, so as to foster thinking in the language, and in this way to acquire real fluency. See ahead:- **Learning the target language in the language itself.**

CHAPTER 5.
A BETTER UNDERSTANDING OF THE FOREIGN LANGUAGE.

5.1 The difference between Literal and Literary English translations. Knowing which to use and when.

A literal English translation is one that is as reasonably close as possible to the meaning of the original foreign text, subject of course to the constraints that inevitably exist whenever any foreign text is translated (see ahead: - **A Mechanical Fallacy**). English words with the nearest meaning to the foreign word are employed in the translation and no attempt is made to substitute English metaphors or expressions for foreign ones. Nothing is left out "because it is obvious"; nothing is changed because "that is what an English speaker would say in the circumstances" and nothing is added, "so as to make the English sound better". No attempt is made to produce good English writing.

A stricter word by word English literal translation, which would not usually be necessary, would even endeavour to set out the English with a word order as close as possible to the foreign text; even if the English would thereby lose some of it's usual word order; and might also include words that would be superfluous in English.

On the other hand a literary translation is one in which the translator has tried to present the same ideas and detail as the foreign text, more or less faithfully to the spirit of the original, but in the way in which they would appear in well written English prose. Different English expressions and idioms are substituted for foreign ones wherever they would be more appropriate. Difficult or unusual metaphors are often changed to typical but quite different English metaphors: and verb tenses and adjectives may be changed. All this may be quite acceptable in any work that is intended

49

to be purely literary, especially bearing in mind that languages do not always translate comfortably from one to another.

A literary translation however may also be patronising if it strays still further from the original, with changes that are intrusive, unnecessary or pointless. With this type of translation, obvious English words and phrases, that might be provided quite simply and satisfactorily, by a fair translation of words that appear in the foreign version, are passed over, and quite different, sometimes quite inaccurate English words are inserted instead. Entire phrases may be omitted and something quite novel inserted in their place.

Misleading words and phrases may be used. Also the reader may be treated as though of limited ability and unable to understand or appreciate any foreign language metaphors or expressions, and so, in their place, English expressions are given with none of the original foreign flavour and colour whatever. As progress is made in the study of the target language such translations will inevitably be encountered from time to time. Those who translate in this way would appear to be suffering from some sort of false-translator syndrome.

Even more objectionable are translations in which the translator has attempted to demonstrate literary skills that quite evidently are not possessed, by introducing ornate prose and flourishes that leave the original foreign text far away.

Literary translations, especially when patronizing, are the absolute bane of the foreign language student's life. When reading a foreign text and then turning to the English version to learn, to check accuracy, or to translate back into the foreign version, it is most important that the English should not be misleading.

The exact meaning of the foreign words needs to be known so that the study will be as accurate as possible, and so that when the same foreign words and expressions are used again by the student in some other context, they will mean what is intended and not something else. With a literary translation it is impossible to be sure that this will be the case.

It is unfortunate that many English translations of foreign language texts are not to be relied upon for accuracy. And whereas a literary translation may be all very well for those who are merely interested in reading an English version of a foreign book, it will not be satisfactory if it is hoped to use the English text for language study, unless it is accurately faithful to the original.

Accordingly, before placing reliance on any translation of a foreign text into English and especially when using the parallel method, it will be necessary to check the translation carefully to ensure that it is close or literal, either writing out the correct English version in full or applying a pen to the printed version as necessary.

The complete beginner may also like to employ a strict word-by-word literal English translation until accustomed to the foreign word order and sentence structures. As progress is made, the austerity of the word by word literal rule can be relaxed by using more of the usual English structure in place of the foreign syntax; although it should be borne in mind that, when reading in English, the use of a foreign word order will be an aid to adapting to that way of speaking in the foreign language, and in due course to thinking in the language. The individual must find by experience, what is most conducive to his own learning. However it will always be unsatisfactory to leave flowery or misleading English versions un-amended.

The above remarks are aimed at translations from an original foreign text into English. When translating from an original English text into a foreign language the position may be different. Translations into the foreign language for purely literary purposes may fairly allow for reasonable changes of idiom and metaphors where the English does not need to be understood with precision by the general reader who is not trying to learn the English language.

For example, expressions such as "on the dog and bone" and "gone to spend a penny" would be better changed to more easily understood expressions in the foreign language (preferably with the literal words in brackets).

The same is true of puns, the meaning of which will usually be completely lost in translation. But showy or ornate language and misguided attempts to produce what is imagined to be a fine prose style should always be avoided. Finally it should be borne in mind that a foreign person learning English would need to have a literal version; and even to see precise translations in their own language of such words as "on the dog and bone" and "spend a penny", for the same reason that anyone learning a foreign language would want a literal version, if their positions were reversed.

It will be understood that the above advice is only for the benefit of those learning a language. When a good degree of fluency has been achieved, and if for example a professional translation is to be undertaken, quite different considerations will arise, such as the need for absolute accuracy with scientific texts, or with literature the need to present the work with the feel of the original but with comfortably flowing prose. None of this will be of concern when still in the early stages of learning a foreign language.

5.2. A Mechanical foreign language fallacy and how to avoid it.

Any discussion of literal and literary English translations (see above) needs to take into account what might be described as a mechanical fallacy, namely the natural expectation of the beginner that what is said in one language can be translated with simple mechanical accuracy into another. This view is understandable but mistaken, because, except for simple and straightforward expressions, it may not be possible to translate direct meaning.

The difficulty lies in the fact that language is not just a collection of words connected by rules, but a means of expressing ideas; and whilst ideas may be similar in different cultures, they may not be identical. Consequently there may not be an equivalent word in the foreign language for an English word or in English for the foreign word. Likewise there may not even be an equivalent verb tense or other appropriate structure.

Nor may there be an expression in one language that will match with perfect symmetry one to be found in the other. Often the best that can be done is to translate, as closely as possible, the generality of the idea that has been expressed, perhaps with some amplification in brackets.

The mistaken mechanical view of language is inevitably fostered by the necessity, especially in the early stages of learning a language, of acquiring a reasonable vocabulary; and also the desirability of having an English translation (provided in the textbook) of the foreign language texts. Moreover the earliest use of the foreign language when learning will inevitably be simplistic, and give the impression that every expression is like a coin, with the value on the obverse reflected in a translation on the reverse, but being still the same coin with the same value.

The mistaken view may be carried further if there is un-due emphasis on the learning of grammar rather than by learning with reference to the spoken language. Learning with excessive attention to grammar may suggest that the foreign language can be constructed just by applying a set of rules, which of course it cannot. Failure to appreciate this matter will result in greater difficulty when learning the language, as well as stilted and unsatisfactory foreign translations reflecting the English from which they are derived rather than comfortable use of the foreign language.

However none of what has been said above should be allowed to undermine the importance of having a literal English translation of any foreign text for learning purposes, although in practice it may be difficult, for the reasons explained, to achieve it fully. Some compromise may be necessary; but wherever that is so, the simplest expressions, and the most straightforward translations practical in the circumstances will be preferable.

Suggestions: -

** Being aware of the problem will help to avoid a mechanical approach to the language.

** Grammar should not be regarded as a tool to engineer a translation. It should be employed as a guide to gain an understanding of the language, and to help to produce comfortable and correct use of the language.

** English translations for language learning purposes should, as far as practical, be close or literal so as to emphasis the original foreign construction and to aid thinking in foreign language terms. It does not matter if the English version is awkward provided that it reflects the foreign text. What matters, is that the target language translations into English are correct, not that they are comfortably expressed.

** Idiomatic expressions and usage in the foreign language should be embraced and not avoided.

** Words to be learned should be those that are in common use in the foreign language; and learning them by the group method (see ahead **How to memorize vocabulary: the Group Method**) will assist an approach the foreign language in its own terms.

** When translating from English, or trying to speak in the language, it is better not to look up the foreign words frequently in a dictionary, but instead to use what has already been learned and understood.

** It is preferable to try not to think in English and then to translate into the foreign language, but instead to try to think and speak in the foreign language. This is not easy for the beginner but it is the ideal to be aimed for, and with practice will be achieved.

5.3 How to use curiosity to enhance foreign language learning.

Curiosity is a spur to learning and concentration. A desire to know more about the background to the target language, about the people who speak it and their way of life, will help to maintain the motivation necessary for study.

Curiosity can be improved by:

** Taking time to discover more about the countries where the language is spoken: the people who speak it and their culture.

** Keeping a scrapbook of items relating to the language and the countries where it is spoken, e.g. press cuttings, advertisements, product labels etc.

** Writing to target language pen pals about their way of life.

** Visiting cultural or trade exhibitions with connections to the countries where the language is spoken.

** Taking an interest in the origins of the language, it's history, it's development, and it's relationship with other languages.

5.4 How to develop deeper and better concentration for foreign language study.

Most people will have found sometimes, having just read a chapter of the course book and gone over the explanations and examples provided, that little or no memory remains of what should have been learned. This annoying occurrence is caused largely by a lack of concentration during the study period. If the whole of the attention is not focused on the text it will not be learned satisfactorily. But with good concentration it should be possible to study and digest any coursework well.

Suggestions for achieving better concentration: -

** At the beginning of a study session, warming up the mind and encouraging the mood for concentration, by going over briefly the last lesson that was worked on.

** Over-viewing the particular chapter or section intended for the days study. This will be an application to the day's study, of the overview technique recommended for the whole course. Skim reading; making a note of the headings the general principals covered and the examples; and then reading quickly over the exercises. If using audio then skim reading the transcript. Then beginning the detailed study.

** Taking notes. When taking notes it is not possible to imagine that studying is going on whilst in reality the mind is elsewhere. When taking written notes, if they begin to tail off, you will be prompted to pay more attention. Also note taking requires active rather than passive thought. This is because the notes, which must never be simple reproductions from the text being studied, should be the essentials set out in one's own words. Note taking is also helpful for any aspects of language learning that are found difficult, because understanding is improved by the heightened concentration that note taking stimulates.

Note taking can be in one of two forms. Either notes for the permanent notebook on the foreign language, or temporary notes made merely to assist understanding and concentration. The latter having served their purpose may be thrown away after the study period.

** Asking questions and looking for answers. If the study is undertaken whilst at the same time looking for answers to specific questions or problems, greater attention will be paid to what is read. For example: how might what is being studied at that moment be used or adapted in particular situations? How might the material be used in a conversation? How can the exercises - already glimpsed or even attempted - be tackled? What other sentences could be made up with the new tenses learnt? Etc.

** Using recitation techniques at the end of each page. I.E. Covering over the page and trying to recollect what has just been read, then checking for accuracy. If there has been an error, then repeating the reading and trying again.

** Reading aloud during study and in particular reading aloud all foreign language text and examples.

** Taking regular breaks so as to stay fresh and alert when studying.

** Studying when properly awake and not when tired.

CHAPTER 6.
MEMORIZING VOCABULARY SUCCESSFULLY.

6.1 Memorizing vocabulary: How to prepare.

A good preparation can be made for memorizing vocabulary by a preliminary period of reading, listening to, writing out and speaking aloud the selected words or phrases. This makes the work of memorizing easier when it is started, because the words will already have been recorded a little in the mind, as a result of the advance preparation. These preliminary activities are forms of repetition but the following methods will ensure that the repetition is active-

** Listening to the words on the audio whilst reading them at the same time.

** Speaking the words aloud whilst writing them out.

** Listening to the words being spoken without reading them.

** Speaking the words aloud whilst reading them without listening to the audio.

** Speaking the words aloud whilst at the same time listening to them - I.E. simultaneously with the audio speaker.

** Writing out short sentences using the words to be learned.

** Repeating each of the above several times.

6.2 How to memorize vocabulary: A basic method.

A basic and frequently used method of learning vocabulary is to take a simple list of individual foreign words with their English translation alongside. Gender is detailed as necessary so that the gender will be learned with the word.

After a period of study the foreign words are covered over and an attempt is made to recall the foreign word for each English word - (recitation) - and vice versa. The English words could be set out on one side of a flash card and the foreign on the other. As the list of words is worked through the card is flipped over to check accuracy or to refresh the memory.

Although this method involves both repetition and recitation, memorizing words this way is more difficult than by using other methods. The fact that the words in the list may generally have no connection with one another, that is to say, are not linked together in any way, except perhaps by some theme, makes the method dry work for the student. It is best to consider the other memorizing techniques, before undue amounts of time are spent with this method.

Other points when learning vocabulary: -

** Concentrate on memorizing words in general use and of practical benefit in real speech

** As a beginner it is best to avoid words that are academic, scientific, technical, scholarly, or archaic. It is possible to get by nearly all the time without any of them, just as one can in English. If a specialized vocabulary is needed, wait until the language study is well advanced before bothering about learning it.

6.3 How to memorize vocabulary: Using simple connections.

A good step up from the basic method of vocabulary learning previously described is to make a note (alongside the English word on the list being memorized) of any reasons that the foreign word may be recognizable; perhaps the language has common roots with English; or perhaps it is a loan word; or perhaps it has some other relationship or similarity (if it is not too distant). When curious about words and interested in their derivation and background it will obviously be easier to find a connection in this way. An English etymological dictionary or one in the target language may be of help with this method.

Looking for a connection, thinking about it and jotting it down on the vocabulary list are all things which will increase attention and concentration and make it easier in future to remember the words being learned.

6.4 How to memorize vocabulary: The Memory Link Method.

The method for memorizing vocabulary described here is not new. In fact it has roots in antiquity, being based on memory techniques developed by the ancient Greeks. For all that, the method is hardly known at all, although it is so effective that, on first discovering it, any student will surely feel,

"Like stout Cortez when with eagle eyes

He stared at the Pacific and all his men

Look'd at each other with a wild surmise

Silent, upon a peak in Darien."

The technique requires the creation in the memory of an unlikely and indirect (but memorable) association or link between the foreign word and the English word. This is a form of artificially constructed memory known as a 'memoria technica'.

There are two stages to the technique.

First: Some sound or spelling is looked for in the foreign word that triggers a thought in whole or in part of an English word. This English word, which we will call a 'linkword', will be used to bring the foreign word and the translation together. Note: what is wanted as a linkword is not a translation, nor anything that necessarily has anything even remotely to do with the meaning of the foreign word. An English word is to be found (but not the translated meaning) that triggers a thought of the foreign word for some reason, however illogical that reason may be.

Second: An absurd or ludicrous or humorous or vulgar picture bringing together the linkword and the English translation is visualized.

This visualization will only exist in the mind; so it can be, and needs to be, as extraordinary as it can be made. As the visualization is made the foreign word and the English word will be welded together in the memory.

In brief then:

1. Foreign word: a linkword is found.

2. An absurd picture between the linkword and the English word is visualized.

Having the linkword assists what might otherwise be a good deal more difficult; namely the memorization of the meaning of a foreign word. In future the translation of the foreign word will be recalled because the linkword will prompt the foreign word, and in this way will return the memory to the English word; and vice versa.

Here are some examples that will make the method perfectly clear. They are limited for convenience to French, German and Spanish words, although the technique will work with any language. Note how the linkword does not even have to be a very good match with the foreign word for the technique to work.

French word: MOULES

English word; MUSSELS

Linkword: MULES

Possible visualization: Picture mules fighting giant mussels

French word: COTE

English word: HILL

Linkword: COAT

Possible visualization: Picture a giant coat being spread over a hillside.

French word: LAPIN

English word: RABBIT

Linkword: LAPPING or LAPWING

Possible visualization: Picture a rabbit lapping water, or a rabbit flying with a lapwing.

French word: FILS

English word: SON

Linkword: FEAST (good sound but not the T) or FILLS (poor sound but close spelling)

Possible visualization: Picture a son at a feas(t). Remember that it is not tea (t) and then the pronunciation will be correct as well - perhaps he fills himself with food.

French word: CHEVAL

English word: HORSE

Linkword: SHOVEL

Possible visualization: Picture a horse laden with a giant shovel.

Spanish Word: LORO

English Word: PARROT

Linkword: LORRY

Possible visualization: Picture a parrot driving a lorry.

Spanish word: BUTACA

English Word: ARMCHAIR

Linkword: BUTTOCKS

Possible visualization: Picture enormous buttocks squeezing into an armchair.

Spanish word: MONO

English word: MONKEY

Linkword: MONO-(CYCLE)

Possible visualization: Imagine a monkey riding a mono-(cycle).

Spanish word: ARROJAR

English word: TO THROW

Linkword: A ROCK HARD

Possible visualization: Imagine a rock being thrown hard.

Spanish word: RISCO

English word: CLIFF OR CRAG

Linkword: RISKY

Possible visualization: Imagine a risky climb up a cliff or crag.

German word: RATHAUS

English word: TOWN HALL

Linkword: RAT HOUSE

Possible visualization: Picture rats swarming into a town hall.

German word: HUPE

English word: HORN

Linkword: HOOP

Possible visualization: Picture a child's hoop that is being played like a horn.

German word: GABEL

English word: FORK

Linkword: GABLE

Possible visualization: Picture the gable of a house made of forks

German word: MANTEL

English word: COAT

Linkword: MANTLE

Possible visualization: Imagine a mantelpiece made of coats

German word: BILD

English word: PICTURE

Linkword: BUILD

Possible visualization: Imagine a builder building with pictures.

The best memory visualizations are those that are not tame or small in scale in the mind, but large or giant, absurd and forceful. In fact, the more ridiculous, the better. No one else will see or even know about the visualizations that you make, so the imagination can be as vulgar and as extraordinary as desired. For example, images prompted by words such as bursting, crashing, merging and smashing, will inspire good mental pictures.

It must always be remembered that the linkword does not have anything to do with the translation or definition of the foreign word. The object of the linkword is to provide a sound or spelling that will trigger the memory of the original foreign word, and also give the means to make an extraordinary visualization with the English word.

It follows that the linkword will be adequate provided it has just enough about it to recall the foreign word. Accordingly the correct full idea of foreign word can often be transmitted by just a part or approximation of its sound. This alone may be sufficient to act as a prompt to the memory.

What this method does is to release the creative powers of the mind so that they can be used as well as logic and reason in creating a dynamic memory bridge between the foreign word and the English word.

Whilst the making of extraordinary mental images may seem a strange way of memorizing, with the benefit of a little practice it will be seen how easy this method becomes. And once the foreign word has been used sufficiently there will be no need to think about the linkword any more; the foreign word and the English will simply be remembered.

6.5 How to memorize vocabulary: The Group Method.

Another good memorization method is to learn vocabulary not as individual words, but together with other words in phrases and or short sentences.

Learning vocabulary by this method has many advantages over single word memorization: -

** The facts described in the phrase or sentence will be an aid to remembering the foreign words used. Likewise the use of words with others builds up associations between each of them in the memory, making all of them easier to recall.

** Word patterns and the rhythms of the phrases and sentences are unconsciously absorbed, again making all the words used easier to remember.

** Conversational skills are being developed from the earliest stages of learning, and this is an encouragement also to begin to think in the language.

** The phrases and sentences are quickly picked up and can then be used either as they are, in speaking the language, or adapted by the substitution of some words.

E.G. "Is there a bank near here?"

"Is there a post office near here?"

"There is a post office over there."

** Some grammar in the sentences will be unconsciously absorbed, allowing for a degree of analogous application in other sentences/situations.

This method of vocabulary learning helps the development of an intuitive feel for the language. Language is not just a collection of words. We do not speak by searching the memory for each of the various words

64

required, working out how they are affected by grammar, and finally, bit by bit, putting a sentence together. Instead we draw on the stock of both word patterns and vocabulary in the mind and adapt them intuitively. We are prompted as necessary by a knowledge of grammar, which is instinctive in the case of our mother tongue, and which with practice and experience has created a feel for what sounds right, and so may be used, or, as the case may be, sounds incorrect, and so should be avoided. This is what will be fostered, by using the group method.

The above comments should suffice as assurance that there are many reasons why the group method is so useful.

Phrases or sentences that are not too long, are best. If need be sentences can be broken up into shorter and more digestible parts. Also the phrases or sentences should preferably be interesting, and ideally they should run on from one to another following a common idea or story. This makes them more easily memorized than those that are not related or connected. Course book conversations and texts should generally provide good sources for memorizing vocabulary in this way.

CHAPTER 7.

THE SECRETS OF

THE MULTI-LINGUISTS.

7.1 How Queen Elizabeth 1 learned to speak five foreign languages fluently.

Queen Elizabeth 1 (1533 to 1603) learnt to speak Spanish, French, Italian, Latin and ancient Greek fluently. Her tutors were William Grindall, a fellow of Cambridge University, and after he died, Roger Ascham, the famous humanist Tudor scholar, also from Cambridge University.

Ascham was particularly influential in Elizabeth's education. His method of teaching foreign languages was not to follow the then traditional practice of concentrating mostly on the rules of grammar, and neglecting the active use of the language, but to encourage learning by taking texts in the target language and translating them back to back. First, a text from the foreign language was translated into English. Next, with the foreign version put away, the student attempted to translate the English back into the foreign language.

The two were then compared, corrected as necessary; and points and rules of grammar extracted explained by the teacher, so that they were properly understood by the student. This was the method, known as double translation that has already been discussed above, which was followed by then Princess Elizabeth.

In his advocacy of this method, with the study of grammar dependent upon use of the language, and not as a preliminary to the study of the language, and certainly not to be treated as almost the only object for the student, Roger Ascham was far ahead of his time. And his approach is one that will reward anyone learning a foreign language today.

The young Princess Elizabeth also improved her Latin by exchanging letters in the language with both her father Henry VIII and her brother Edward: an example of the pen pal method.

Even after she became Queen, Elizabeth continued to keep up her languages, often translating works from Greek and Latin into English; and in addition composing and speaking in Latin. Also she composed poems and prayers in both Greek and Latin. Ascham said of her "Yea, I believe, that beside her perfect readiness in Latin, Italian, French, and Spanish, she readeth here now at Windsor more Greek every day than some prebendary of the Church doth read Latin in a whole week."

There is a pleasant story of Elizabeth's reply to the Polish ambassador who had criticized her policy regarding the English war with Spain. The ambassador after being received at court, had launched into a critique of English policy as to the war, all delivered in Latin, the diplomatic language of the time, that he read out from a written script he had brought with him.

The court and the Polish ambassador were astonished when Elizabeth replied to him at some length in unprepared Latin, rebuking him and his King for the impertinence they had shown. William Cecil, Elizabeth's Secretary of State, afterwards said that her reply had been "the best answer in extempore Latin that I have ever heard".

A particular advantage for Elizabeth, with her skill in five languages, was that she could speak directly to ambassadors and visitors from many other countries without the need for interpreters.

7.2 George Borrow: How this remarkable multi-linguist became fluent in numerous languages.

The learning of different foreign languages was a lifelong interest for the nineteenth century writer and adventurer George Borrow (1803 to 1881) who taught himself to speak over thirty. While still a young boy he mixed with gypsies and learned to speak their language, Romany. As an adult his knowledge of this strange tongue nearly cost him his life when two or three gypsies, who were frightened that a 'Gorgio' who could speak their language, would discover their secrets, tried to murder him.

He survived and later in life he produced a Gypsy word-book and description of the Romany language: Romano Lavo-Lil. He also translated St. Luke's Gospel into the Gypsy language. In Ireland as a child he additionally learned Irish, not at his school, but from other children.

At the age of just sixteen whilst articled to a Norfolk solicitor, George Borrow often spent his time, not studying law, but teaching himself Welsh. The way in which he did so was to study Milton's Paradise Lost alongside Owen Pugh's translation of the same work into Welsh: an example of learning by the parallel method. His study based on these texts was backed up by conversation practice with a Welsh ostler in Norwich.

Learning a language mainly by studying parallel texts and without other guidance in the form of the course books and audio etc. that are now readily available, would not now normally be recommended. But the use of parallel texts coupled with other methods would be an excellent approach.

Inevitably Borrow soon abandoned the law as a career; and by the age of thirty he had not distinguished himself in anything except the learning of languages. Then, due to his knowledge of Russian, the Bible Society offered him a job in Russia dealing with the preparation of an edition of the Gospels in Manchu, a language of which Borrow knew absolutely nothing. The offer was conditional on his learning the Manchu language within just six months, a time scale that would make most people give up at once.

Borrow's only resources for this formidable undertaking were a copy of St. Matthew's Gospel printed in Manchu, a Manchu-French dictionary and The Alphabet Mantchou Francois. Later he acquired a further book, Von Klaproth's Chrestomathie Mandchou: a collection of writings in the Manchou language. He was unable to obtain a Manchu grammar. Within nineteen weeks of concentrated study he had succeeded in mastering the language. He was given the job by the Bible Society, went to Russia and was triumphant in producing the desired edition of the New Testament in Manchu.

After returning from Russia, his ability with so many languages gained Borrow further employment with the Bible Society which sent him to Spain where he had the many extraordinary adventures, dangerous travels, dealings with gypsies, threats of death, clashes with the authorities and even a period of imprisonment, that are recounted in his fascinating book

'The Bible In Spain', and which made him such a famous agent of the Bible Society.

For more information on Borrow, his languages and his adventures, the reader is referred to his published works and in particular to Lavengro, The Bible In Spain, Wild Wales, and The Letters of George Borrow to the British and Foreign Bible Society.

7.3 Charlotte Bronte's foreign language learning methods.

An impressive linguist with a keen interest in foreign languages, Charlotte Bronte (1816 to 1855) was fluent in Latin, Greek, French and German. What is known or can be deduced about her methods for learning languages will give help and inspiration to anyone wanting to achieve success with their own chosen foreign language.

For example, amongst Bronte's techniques for learning languages were, as will be seen, the regular translation of foreign language poetry into English and the memorization of up to a page of foreign language text each day. These are valuable methods for anyone studying a language to adopt.

Bronte hoped to start her own school and in order to perfect her use of French and German for the purpose, she bravely decided, at the age of 26, to go with her sister Emily to a girl's school in Brussels. The school was the Pensionnat Heger, and it was able to give Charlotte Bronte and her sister an adult education in languages and other skills.

Some time after they had begun their studies, the school proprietor, M. Heger, determined that he would not teach formal grammar and syntax, but would instead assist them to read great literary works in the studied languages; and by their study of these works and the styles of their authors, to bring both Charlotte and Emily, to fluency in the languages.

The following extract from Jane Eyre by Bronte gives us a very good account of some of her learning methods.

"Fortunately I had had the advantage of being taught French by a French lady; and as I had always made a point of conversing with Madame Pierrot as often as I could, and had, besides, during the last seven years,

learnt a portion of French by heart daily - applying myself to take pains with my accent, and imitating as closely as possible the pronunciation of my teacher - I had acquired a certain degree of readiness and correctness in the language, and was not likely to be much at a loss with Mademoiselle Adela"

A further extract from Bronte's 'Jane Eyre', where she is talking to St. John Rivers gives us another insight into her ideas.

"Jane, what are you doing?"

"Learning German."

"I want you to give up German and learn Hindustani".

"You are not in earnest?"

"In such earnest that I must have it so; and I will tell you why."

Rivers goes on to explain that Hindustani is the language he is himself studying; that as he advances, he is apt to forget the commencement; that it would assist him greatly to have a pupil with whom he might go over the elements, and so fix them thoroughly in his mind.

Having a pupil with whom to go over the elements of the language would give the same benefits as having a study friend.

This extract from Charlotte Bronte's 'The Professor' is clearly based on her experiences.

"... There were two gentlemen talking in French; impossible to follow their rapid utterance, or comprehend much of the purport of what they said, yet French, in the mouths of Frenchmen, or Belgians (I was not then sensible of the horrors of the Belgian accent) was music to my ears. One of these gentlemen presently discerned me to be an Englishman from the fashion in which I addressed the waiter; for I would persist in speaking French in my execrable South of England style, though the man understood English. The gentleman, after looking towards me once or twice politely accosted me in very good English; I remember I wished to God that I could speak French as well; his fluency and correct pronunciation impressed me for the first time with a due notion of the

70

cosmopolitan character of the capital I was in; it was my first experience of that skill in living languages I afterwards found to be so general in Brussels".

Extracts from Mrs. Gaskells Life of Charlotte Bronte

Further illustration of the methods of the Bronte's in the learning of foreign languages, is found in the following extracts from the biography of Charlotte Bronte by her friend Elizabeth Gaskell.

"......it was Emily who made all the bread for the family; and anyone passing by the kitchen door might have seen her studying German out of an open book, propped up before her as she kneaded the dough; but no study however interesting, interfered with the goodness of the bread......."

From a letter by Charlotte Bronte recorded in the biography:

"I have got another bale of French books from G. containing upwards of forty volumes. I have read about half. They are like the rest, clever, wicked, sophistical, and immoral. The best of it is, they give one a thorough idea of France and Paris, and are the best substitute for French conversation that I have met with".

The following extracts deal with some of Charlotte Bronte's time at The Pensionnat Heger:

"M. Heger's account is that they knew nothing of French. I suspect they knew as much (or as little), for all conversational purposes, as any English girls do, who have never been abroad, and have only learnt the idioms and pronunciations from an Englishwoman............"

"After consulting with his wife, M. Heger told them that he meant to dispense with the old method of grounding in grammar, vocabulary, etc., and to proceed to a new plan--something similar to what he had occasionally adopted with the elder among his French and Belgian pupils. He proposed to read to them some of the masterpieces of the most celebrated French authors (such as Casimir de la Vigne's poem on the

71

'Death of Joan of Arc', parts of Bossuet, the Admirable translation of the noble of St. Ignatius to the Roman Christians in the Bibliotheque Choisie des Peres de l'Eglise, etc.), and after having thus impressed the complete effect of the whole, to analyse the parts of them, pointing out in what such or such an author excelled, and where there were blemishes. He believed that he had to do with pupils capable, from their ready sympathy with the intellectual, the refined, the polished or the noble, of catching the echo of a style, and so reproducing their own thoughts in somewhat similar manner".

Charlotte Bronte's comments on M. Heger's methods are set out in the next extract of another of her letters recorded in the biography.

"M. Heger......a man of power as to mind, but very choleric and irritable in temperament. He is very angry with me just at present, because I have written a translation, which he chose to stigmatise as 'peu correct'. He did not tell me so, but wrote the word on the margin of my book, asked, in a brief stern phrase, how it happened that my compositions were always better than my translations? Adding, that the thing seemed to him inexplicable. The fact is, some weeks ago, in a high-flown humour, he forbade me to use either dictionary or grammar in translating the most difficult English compositions into French. This makes the task rather arduous, and compels me every now and them to introduce an English word, which nearly plucks the eyes out of his head when he sees it. Emily and he don't draw well together at all. Emily works like a horse, and she has had great difficulties to contend with - far greater than I have had. Indeed those who come to a French school for instruction ought previously to have acquired a considerable knowledge of the French language, otherwise they will lose a great deal of time, for the course of instruction is adapted to natives and not to foreigners; and in these large establishments they will not change their ordinary course for one or two strangers. The few private lessons that M. Heger has vouchsafed to give us are, I suppose to be considered a great favour; and I can perceive they have already excited much spite and jealousy in the school".

Mrs. Gaskell's comments on the method of M. Heger are as follows.

"The passage in this letter where M. Heger is represented as prohibiting the use of dictionary or grammar refers, I imagine, to the time I have mentioned, when he determined to adopt a new method of instruction in the French language, of which they were to catch the spirit and rhythm rather from the ear and the heart, as its noblest accents fell upon them, than by over-careful and anxious study of its grammatical rules. It seems to me a daring experiment on the part of their teacher; but doubtless he knew his ground, and that it answered is evident in the composition of some of Charlotte's devoirs written about this time".

An incident in Charlotte's life after her return to England: -

"On her return from......short visit of three weeks to her friend she travelled with a gentleman in the railway carriage, whose features and bearing betrayed him, in a moment, to be a Frenchman. She ventured to ask him if such was not the case; and, on his admitting it, she further inquired if he had not spent a considerable time in Germany, and was answered that he had; her quick ear detected something of the thick guttural pronunciation, which, Frenchmen say, they are able to discover even in the grandchildren of their countrymen who have lived any time beyond the Rhine."

A brief but revealing remark in the biography: -

Charlotte had retained her skill in the language by the habit of memorizing texts in French which she speaks of to M. Heger as follows: -

" Je crains beacoup d'oublier le francais--j'apprends tous les jours une demie page de francais par coeur, et j'ai grand plaiser a apprendre cette lecon".

The above extracts gleaned from Mrs. Gaskell's biography and from Charlotte Bronte's own works, are all too short, and how helpful it would be if the language learning techniques of such determined and successful linguists as Charlotte Bronte and her sister could be known in more detail.

Nonetheless many useful insights into the language methods of the Bronte's can be obtained from the extracts: -

** Taking every opportunity to press on with the learning. Where practical some study is undertaken even whilst doing household chores.

** Reading books in the language to maintain interest in the language and keep the subject alive, especially when there are no other ways to practice. Reading is regarded as "the best substitute for French conversation".

** Travelling to a country where there are ample opportunities for speaking the foreign language and being immersed in the subject.

** After an initial period of learning, trying to catch the "rhythm rather from the ear", than from the study of rules in books. To put the matter another way, putting aside the props of dictionary etc., using simply what has been learned so as to gain confidence and ability, and being prepared to abandon "over-careful and anxious study of .... grammatical rules". This does not of course mean having no regard for grammar, but using what has been learned as correctly as may be practical and not worrying about perfection.

** Seizing the moment and speaking the language when the chance presents itself, as for example when the Frenchman in the railway carriage is addressed.

** Regularly memorizing by heart passages in the foreign language.

** Taking pains to imitate the correct pronunciation for the language and to acquire the right accent.

7.4 Roger Ascham and "The Scholemaster": The methods of an inspired teacher of foreign languages.

Roger Ascham (1515 to 1568), the tutor appointed, as mentioned above, to teach the future Queen Elizabeth 1, was a Yorkshire man, educated privately until the age of fifteen when he was sent to St. John's College, Cambridge. He applied himself with great energy to languages and especially to the study of ancient Greek. It need hardly be added that he spoke fluently the languages that he taught Elizabeth.

In 1545 Ascham came to the attention of Henry VIII after writing a book about archery that he had dedicated to Henry. Three years later he was

74

invited to come to Court as the tutor to Prince Edward, and later as tutor to Queen Elizabeth (then Princess Elizabeth). Subsequently he was appointed Latin Secretary first to Edward VI, and later to Queen Mary, and finally to Queen Elizabeth. He also had a period as secretary to Sir Richard Morisine who was appointed ambassador to Charles V. This provided him with opportunities to travel in France, Germany and Italy.

As a noted Renaissance scholar and an able teacher Ascham was invited to write a book dealing with the correct way to teach children. His response was the "The Scholemaster", which was published after his death.

When he died suddenly in 1568, Elizabeth said of him "I would rather have cast ten thousand pounds in the sea than be parted from my Ascham".

Set out following, are some extracts from The Scholemaster that are relevant to the teaching of languages.

** On double translation:

"..the childe must take a paper booke, and sitting in some place, where no man shall prompt him, by himselfe, let him translate into Englishe his former lesson. Then showing it to his master, let the master take from him his latin booke, and pausing an houre, at the least, then let the childe translate his owne Englishe into latin againe, in another paper booke. When the childe bringeth it, turned into latin, the master must compare it .... and laie them both together; and where the childe doth well, ...let the master praise him, and saie here ye do well. For I assure you, there is no such whetstone, to sharpen a good witte and encourage a will to learninge, as is praise".

** On the rules of grammar:

"In these fewe lines I have wrapped up the most tedious part of Grammer: also the ground of almost all the Rewles, that are so busilie taught by the Master, and so hardlie learned by the Scholer, in all common scholes: which after this sort, the master shall teach without all error, and the scholer shall learn without great paine: the master being led by so sure a guide, and the scholer being brought into so plaine and easy a waie. And therefore, we do not contemne Rewles, but we gladly teach Rewles: and

75

teach them, more plainlie, sensiblie, and orderlie, than they be commonlie taught in common Scholes. For when the Master shall compare Tullies booke with his (the) Scholers translation, let the Master, at the first, lead and teach his Scholer, to joyne the Rewles of his Grammer booke, with the examples of his present lesson, until the Scholer, by him selfe, be able to fetch out of his Grammer, every Rewle, for every Example: so, As the Grammer booke be ever in the Scholers hand, and also used of him, as a Dictionarie, for every present use. This is a lively and perfite waie of teaching of Rewles: where the common waie in common Scholes, to read the Grammer alone by it selfe, is tedious for the Master, hard for the Scholer, colde and uncomfortable for them bothe".

** On the example of Queen Elizabeth:

"And a better, and nerer example herein, may be, our most noble Queene Elizabeth, who never toke yet, Greeke nor Latin Grammer in her hand, after the first declining of a nowne and a verbe, but onely by this double translating of Demosthenes and Socrates dailie without missing every forenone, for the space of a yeare or two, hath atteyned to such a perfite understanding in both the tonges and to such a readie utterance of the Latin, and that with such a judgement, as they be few in nomber in both the universities, or els where in England, that be, in both tonges, comparable with her Majestie".

7.5 The amazing multi-lingual Cardinal.

Cardinal Guiseppe Mezzofanti (1774 to 1849), the son of a poor carpenter, learned to speak over forty languages fluently. This remarkable Catholic clergyman made the study of different languages his hobby and, incredibly, managed to learn all his languages without ever travelling away from his home country Italy. In addition to the forty languages, that he spoke fluently, he was conversant to a good standard with at least thirty other languages, as well as numerous dialects.

Native speakers of his studied languages, who spoke with him, invariably confirmed his perfect command of their language, and the accuracy of his accent in the language. He is properly acclaimed as one of the greatest multi-linguists ever.

76

Unfortunately a comprehensive understanding of Mezzofanti's methods is not available, not least because he left no written account as to how he set about learning languages. However a good deal of information is nonetheless available, derived mainly from his reported conversations with friends and academics, and his observed practice with regard to studying. From these sources a substantial, albeit incomplete, picture can be put together.

To begin with when learning a languages, Mezzofanti would concentrate on a list of some 500 words that he had identified as being the most important and indispensable in any language. Likewise conversational forms were studied with assistance being sought where possible from those who spoke only the studied language, and especially from children for the benefit of their simplicity of understanding and expression. All this was routinely committed to memory.

Also he made a point of gathering together a good collection of texts, vocabulary lists, reading books and dictionaries in the language. All the available resources were thus brought to bear on the subject. With the benefit of these Mezzofanti would then write out all that he needed to remember and again set about memorizing it diligently.

It was the view of Mezzofanti that the number of really essential points that had to be mastered in a language, was not substantial. These had to be identified and the greatest attention given to them, but once they had been tackled he believed that the rest of the language would follow with great facility. Mezzofanti is reported as being able always to secure quickly a mastery of the essentials; because by reason of his powerful analytical faculties he could seize upon the whole system of the studied language, giving himself in this way an overall understanding of it's form, structure, idiom, genius, and spirit. In effect he commanded an overview of the language as a preliminary.

Mezzofanti did not achieve his linguistic successes without regular studying. There is some evidence that his memory powers were rather better than average; and he appears to have had good recall in many other subjects apart from languages. But time, attention and systematic work were invariably devoted to each language that he wished to learn.

He also realized the value of utilizing small amounts of time that might otherwise be frittered away. Whenever he had even just a few moments to spare from his other duties, he would immediately take up his books and language notes and apply himself to them assiduously. His time was never wasted and frequent studying rather than unusual memory power was an important feature of his success with languages.

Amongst the other studying techniques employed by Mezzofanti was the regular and systematic translating and composing of texts in both prose and poetry in the studied language. Energy, time and attention were devoted to these various elements of learning. Additionally, Mezzofanti was able, from practice and self discipline, to have a high degree of concentration in his periods of studying, during which he was able to focus exclusively on what was to be learned and to block out distractions of whatever nature, even during the shortest periods of study.

Mezzofanti was noted for his invariably excellent pronunciation in each of the languages that he spoke. His accent was always reported to be flawless. In this, he was undoubtedly assisted by having an extremely accurate ear. This permitted him readily to catch the sounds, rhythms and peculiar intonations of a language.

But to catch the sounds he had first to hear them; and Mezzofanti's practice, of taking every opportunity of talking to native speakers in their own language, is well known. He preferred always those who spoke no other language, and was never deterred by feelings of awkwardness.

Mezzofanti was fortunate in having plentiful access to speakers of other languages. As a Catholic priest in Italy he would have better opportunities than most for meeting speakers of his numerous languages; many of whom were religious workers who had lived in other countries, and there were native speakers of different languages from numerous parts of the world.

Moreover the hospitals in Bologna, his home town and where a good part of his life was spent, had patients who had come from all over Europe as a result of the wars in Napoleonic times. In performing religious duties there as a visiting clergyman Mezzofanti was again provided with excellent opportunities of meeting, talking with and learning from native speakers of many languages.

Later, when Mezzofanti was a Cardinal and living in Rome, where there were invariably visitors from all over the world, the opportunities of meeting speakers of different languages were greatly multiplied. Also whilst at Rome he made visits to the College for foreign missionaries at Naples with the particular object of learning Chinese.

Lastly it is known that Mezzofanti made a habit of thinking constantly, speaking as it were to himself, in the languages which he was learning; and in this way he enjoyed the benefit of practising conversation even when on his own.

Mezzofanti was a popular and well-loved priest, holding a variety of important academic and religious posts during his life. He became known, not surprisingly, as the confessor of foreigners, because of the spiritual aid he was able, with his knowledge of numerous languages, to give to so many from different parts of the world. His move to Rome at the express request of Pope Pius VII was made in 1814 and in 1838 he was created Cardinal. He died in 1848.

A pious and kindly man renowned for his outgoing, friendly and modest nature, his studious habits, and for his delight in adding each new language to his amazing collection, Mezzofanti is a source of inspiration to everyone who wishes to learn a foreign language. He would surely be an excellent candidate to be one of the patron saints of linguists if the Church were to consider that he satisfied the criteria for canonisation.

7.6 The secrets of the multi-linguists.

In this book there has been space to mention only a few multi-linguists. But although the number is modest, an examination of what is known of their learning methods reveals a number of interesting points.

** Memory ability.

Some multi-linguists have undoubtedly enjoyed great powers of memory. Borrow for example is known to have had a quite exceptionally powerful memory, and possessed an ability to recall far beyond what would be considered normal. His memory may even have been eidetic. It might be expected that he would be a better linguist than Mezzofanti, who although he is considered to have had a good memory, is not spoken of as having a power of recall that might be compared with that of Borrow.

However whilst Borrow spoke about thirty languages, Mezzofanti spoke approximately forty fluently, together with a substantial further number of languages - at least thirty - not quite so perfectly, and numerous dialects. Moreover Borrow's command of languages has been criticised as not being always perfect, with occasional faulty pronunciation. But it was said of Mezzofanti that whoever challenged him in their native tongue would then confirm his complete fluency in the language.

So far as the less formidable linguists we have looked at are concerned, Queen Elizabeth, Charlotte Bronte, and Roger Ascham, none was renowned for extraordinary memory powers. In conclusion it may be said that although heightened memory power is clearly an advantage, it is far from being essential for a linguist, and that many other aspects of language learning are at least as important, if not more so.

It might be added for the comfort of those who may believe themselves to have a poor memory, that good memory can be developed, more than is generally realized, by use of good memory techniques and correct use of the memory based on a knowledge of those techniques. Most people are possessed of far greater memory power than they appreciate, but they do not utilize it due to failure to apply their memory properly.

For this reason complaints as to poor memory may be compared with complaining that a car is too slow whilst always driving in first gear, because the use of the gearbox is not understood. Anyone who doubts the truth of this should revisit How to learn vocabulary: the Memory Link Method; and test themselves by memorizing a number of foreign words using the technique described. A start might be made by using the examples given in the text.

** Plentiful materials.

Mezzofanti made a point of amassing a good collection of grammar books, texts, and lists of vocabulary and phrases with which to learn. With the access that he had to the libraries of Bologna University and those of the Church, it was probably not difficult for him to find what he needed. This may be compared with the problems Borrow faced due to a lack of a grammar book when learning Manchu, and having only a translation of Paradise Lost to rely on when learning Welsh. Queen Elizabeth was supplied with the works of classical authors by Ascham. Likewise Bronte was provided with the works of great authors in the languages she studied. Ample study materials and variety in those materials are self-evidently of great importance in the mastery of a foreign language.

** The Parallel Method.

Parallel texts were certainly employed by Borrow in learning both Manchu and Welsh. The method has much similarity with the double translation method.

** Double translation.

This method, advocated by Roger Ascham, was used by Queen Elizabeth.

** Pronunciation.

Mezzofanti was undoubtedly better placed than most would be linguists of his era because he was able, without having to travel abroad, to meet people from so many different countries. It was by travelling widely that Borrow enjoyed similar advantages with most of his languages, although in learning Manchu he had to study without the help of talking with native speakers. Being able to hear and converse in the language is unquestionably a tremendous aid when learning it. Nowadays of course there is easy access to audio courses, foreign language radio services, DVDs etc.

** Overview.

As has been seen it was the practice of Mezzofanti to grasp the overall structure and theory of the studied language as a preliminary step. The importance and value of this technique has been discussed above. That it is a most advantageous starting point for learning a language cannot be overstated.

** Curiosity.

All the linguists had a fascination for languages and enthusiasm for learning them.

** Effective use of time and regular study.

These two go more or less hand in hand, and each is likely to imply the other. Mezzofanti studied every day using every available scrap of time when he was not otherwise occupied. Borrow when learning Manchu studied unrelentingly, devoting every possible moment to the subject. Bronte also studied every day and likewise Elizabeth studied "dailie without missing every forenone".

** Taking opportunities to practice.

Mezzofanti invariably seized every chance of using the studied language in conversation even from the earliest stages of study and was not deterred by any feelings of awkwardness. Borrow's travels abroad gave him ample opportunities to practice.

** Concentration.

All the linguists were noted for single mindedness in applying themselves to the studied languages with great concentration, and not allowing themselves to be distracted from the desired goal of fluency.

** Self-motivated study.

Again all the linguists were prepared to study on their own, and to devote a good deal of time to private self-motivated study. With the reasonable exception of Elizabeth as a child, who then had tutors, and Bronte to the extent that she went back to school as an adult, they did not need to be directed as to how, when or what to study.

** Active memorizing.

This has certainly been an important feature of learning languages for the multi-linguists, from the memorizing of individual words, idioms and phrases, to the committing of whole pages of foreign texts to memory, as was Bronte's practice. All the linguists willingly devoted the necessary time to memorization.

** Mastery of the basics.

Perfect grammar was not the starting point for either Mezzofanti or Borrow. Both preferred to gain a mastery of basics and the ability to express themselves simply in the language before dealing with more detailed matters. Likewise Ascham's view of grammar was that it should not be a study in itself but a means of understanding the construction of foreign texts and thereby aiding the student in perfecting his own use of the language.

** Thinking in the language.

It was the practice of Mezzofanti to talk to himself in the studied language and this would have been a means of encouraging thought in the language.

** Reading widely in the language.

Charlotte Bronte's Reading practice has been mentioned, and also her bale of forty volumes of French books. "The best substitute for French conversation that I have met with".

Conclusion.

It is impossible to say with certainty what particular methods have been used with consistency by any of the handful of linguists we have looked at, but those methods identified and discussed have certainly been employed to greater or lesser extent as indicated.

Those who wish to learn any foreign language will do well to have regard to the methods of those who have been outstandingly successful in the learning of languages; and moreover to employ as many of those methods as possible in the study of their own target language. A carefully focused study, steadily and consistently approaching the language from several different directions each in turn, with self-discipline and perseverance, is the way that is most likely to produce success.

7.7 How anyone with determination can become a multi-linguist.

Having considered the secrets of the multi-linguists many will ask themselves whether they would be able to become a multi-linguist. The answer must depend upon the degree of commitment that exists. It is one thing to find the time to learn one or two languages, but is there the determination and the self-discipline to give the necessary time to learning several more languages?

Inevitably the amount of time to be devoted would be considerable. A leisurely approach would not be realistic if many languages are to be mastered. With a target of say five foreign languages it would probably be necessary to start a fresh language at least every year. And as the list of languages learned grew longer, more time would have to be given to periodic revision of those already learned.

It certainly would not be an easy undertaking, but with genuine enthusiasm and fascination with languages, as well as a strong desire to learn it would not be impossible for any reasonably educated person to master several foreign languages. It would be essential to apply consistently the methods explained in this book for language learning, and ideally to spend a reasonable amount of time each year with those who spoke only the target language, so as to achieve real fluency.

But with steady application to the endeavour, success could be expected. If the languages are selected from the same group or family as others already learned, the task would be easier. And moreover many linguists take the view that learning each successive language becomes easier as more are added to the list of those that have been learned.

CHAPTER 8.

GAINING CONFIDENCE AND SKILLS IN THE FOREIGN LANGUAGE.

8.1 The use and benefits of analogous application in learning a foreign language.

Language, the use of language, and the use of words in their normal way in speech, has a natural energy that is lost when the language is first dissected and then constructed or reconstructed as a purely grammatical exercise. A language develops because of this natural energy and not because it is conforming to rules of grammar. To put the matter another way, a language is organic will have grown and will continue to grow because of the way that people speak it; and they do not speak it by reference to grammar. They speak the language in a particular way because that is how it feels right or comfortable for them to do so.

Various themes, or patterns, may be identified in the language by grammarians and these are then allowed to crystallize as the rules of grammar for the language. Whilst these rules are of great value, it must always be remembered that the rules extracted in this way are in reality following the development of the language and not creating the language.

In learning a language, even as children, we become unconsciously aware of the energy in the language and of the direction that it leads us. So when a number of sentences or word structures have been acquired it becomes instinctive to apply similar forms elsewhere in the language, even though this may lead sometimes to errors by those who are not experienced with the language, whether they are children learning to speak for the first time, or those learning it as a second language.

Consider for example the child who has learned to say, "he springs"; and "he sprang" and also "he brings". Many parents must then have heard their child say, "he brang", or "he bringed" instead of "he brought". The mistake is sensible and logical; the child has unconsciously formulated a rule as to how to conjugate verbs ending in ING but has not learned the exception. However when the child applying the unconscious rule, says "the telephone rang" it will be correct; and as to saying "he brang", the parent will explain the right verb to the child once or twice, probably without thinking at all about the thought process that led to the mistake, and thereafter the child will get it right.

The application of the form or structure applicable to one expression or phrase in the language to another that is similar, may be described as analogous application; and in our mother language the process is largely unconscious, unless we trouble to think about it. Consider, for example, how we cheerfully and effortlessly adapt nouns for use as verbs, and conjugate them in the required tense without a moments thought.

Those who try to learn a foreign language only by listening and trying to repeat, rely to a great extent, whether they are aware of it or not, on analogous application. The process is unquestionably useful and a valuable part of language learning, although it has serious limitations if other methods of learning to speak the language correctly are not also followed.

For a start, if relying solely on listening and trying to repeat, the benefit of the shortcuts provided by a knowledge of grammar, and a more systematic approach, are missed. Errors are then more likely to become a matter of habit and are then difficult to eradicate. Indeed one may not even become aware of the errors, if only because as an adult it is less likely, for reasons of simple misplaced politeness or indifference, that incorrect speech will be criticized or corrected by others. On the other hand a child would normally be told the right way to speak if a mistake is made.

Moreover a quick ear is often necessary to catch the original on which learning by this method is based, because the chances of a mistake are greater when relying just on what is heard. Another problem is that a substantial range of experience of the language is needful, if learning is to be undertaken just by listening and trying to copy; if relying on analogous application alone for accurate grammar is to produce even passable results; and if mistakes are not to be made as to what is correct speech, as can so easily occur when relying exclusively on this method.

Despite this, it has to be conceded that some people do manage to make progress in mastering a language by simple listening, repeating and trying to adapt what they have learned without any studying. And the obvious benefits of analogous application need not be discounted merely because it is not generally satisfactory as a stand-alone method of learning correct speech in a foreign language.

It is certainly practical and helpful to apply structures that have been learned in one construction in the target language situation to other similar constructions. Knowing this, it will be advantageous, for example, to learn vocabulary in short phrases or sentences; to memorize appropriate texts (this is particularly valuable) and to practice by repeating what is accurately heard spoken by native speakers. And the exercises and texts to be selected for practice should be those most likely to provide the necessary range and experience.

8.2 Staying with a family: how to gain the most from the experience.

Staying with a family in a country where the target language is spoken is one of the best ancillary aids to learning the language that can be had. However there are certain desirable conditions if the experience is to provide the fullest benefit.

** First. It is best that no one in the host family should be able to speak English or even, ideally for that matter, to want to learn it. If English is spoken by the family or by some of them, they will naturally find it irresistible to practice it; and the student, who should be learning their language, may end up involuntarily providing the family with lessons in English. This will especially be the case if the student's own command of the target language is not yet strong.

A similar objection arises if there is to be a student exchange, with some member of the family intended to have a return visit and stay at some stage in the future. It would be hard, and of course discourteous, to refuse to speak any English at all if some member of the family wants to try speaking it a little, or, if they are a bit pushy, speaking it a lot.

It will be preferable to avoid problems of this nature by arranging the stay with a family where there is no prospect of English being spoken. If, the stay is being arranged with the assistance of a language school, appropriate enquiries should be made as to this and "no English to be spoken by the family" requested.

** Second. It will be preferable not to be part of an English group, all of whom are staying in the locality. Inevitably if other English companions are met during the day, English will be spoken with them. How much better it will be if the target language has to be practised with the available native speakers, if only because there is no one else to speak to.

** Third. It is important that the family should really treat the student as one of the family and that he should live with them properly, joining in their activities and being one of the family group; and not be treated merely as a guest would be in an hotel. This can be encouraged if a point is made of helping in the family's home and being available to join in whatever is going on.

Offers should be made to accompany family members when shopping, and to join in with the cooking or the washing up etc. Conversations about themselves and their way of life, their children, their aspirations etc. will all help. In this way there should be plentiful opportunities to hear and speak and learn the target language really thoroughly by constant exposure to it; and every opportunity should be seized.

** Fourth. Active studying of the language is desirable during a stay, with a portion of every day being set aside during which to study some aspect of the language or to revise, or just to memorize more vocabulary to be tried out presently. The combination of studying the target language and being in an environment where the only the target language will be heard and spoken daily can result in remarkable progress in a short time.

8.3 Practicing with native speakers of the foreign language.

Having begun the study of the target language, every opportunity should be taken that presents itself to practice with those who speak the language, but especially with native speakers. Only with those for whom the language is the mother tongue, can one be sure of hearing the authentic accent and intonation. And speaking the language, even if not very well at first, will give confidence that the efforts being made really are worthwhile and are producing results.

It is best not to be confined to just one speaker. Ideally conversation should be with as many as possible so as to provide a good range of different voices, tones, local accents, and different idioms and expressions that may vary from one person to another, and from one region to another.

Finding a native speaker:

** Enquire at local schools and colleges. They may have foreign students or teachers.

** The public library may have details of societies and clubs that can provide contact with native speakers.

Before meeting any stranger the precautions should be taken that would be appropriate with anyone who is unknown. Find out about them, have the first meeting on neutral territory such as a cafe. Take a friend along and if not you are not an adult yourself, be sure always go with an adult etc.

8.4 How to improve conversational skills in the foreign language.

In practical everyday use of the target language, it is necessary to be able to draw down quickly, from memory, the acquired knowledge of the language, to adapt it and to apply it as required in conversation.

When writing in the target language there would be time for reflection, and to consult a dictionary. But when having a conversation this is not possible. The language needs to be more readily to hand, and skill is needed at managing and restructuring phrases so as to produce coherent sentences about the different ideas to be conveyed. To be able to do this satisfactorily, it is a good idea to practice regularly in advance and to make preparation in anticipation of probable conversations that might be had.

Suggestions for imaginary conversations: -

** Telling a bus driver where you want to get out and asking for help with luggage.

** Ordering a special meal in a restaurant to suit a friend's special dietary needs.

** Describing work experience to a prospective employer

** Explaining to a taxi driver that you have changed your mind as to where you want to go.

** Telling a policeman why the accident was the fault of the other driver.

** Telling a friend about a hobby or interest

** Describing the plot of a television play or film that has been seen

** Talking about family, friends, holidays, hobbies and experiences; and asking the other person about the same sort of things.

** Talking about current affairs and topic of interest taken from the newspapers.

** Asking others about themselves, their lives, their activities etc.

Other suggestions: -

** Review conversations had recently about any subject and reproduce them (both parties) in the target language.

** Think about unlikely things as well as the mundane and plan how they might be talked about in the target language.

8.5 Courses at colleges and with tutors: what you need to consider.

As commented previously, learning a language requires a good deal of self-motivated study. There is no substitute for this; but taking a course or working with a private tutor may be considered as well. There are several advantages to doing so:

** The discipline of regular attendance at the course, and the provision of a study structure.

** Regular active practice sessions.

** Encouragement and independent assessment of progress, as well as suggestions from teachers or tutors for further improvement

** Explanations, corrections, and constructive criticism from teachers or tutors

** Opportunities to meet native speakers of the target language and other people learning the same foreign language (opportunities for study friends).

** Total immersion in the language if a residential course is attended (ideally in a country where the language is spoken).

Responsibility for the study, or for success with the study, should never be surrendered to the course or to a teacher, so attendance at the course or time spent with a tutor should be an addition to personal study and not something to be relied instead of working alone. Also lessons with a private tutor, should be switched to a different tutor after a while, as well as alternated between male and female tutors so as to provide experience with a variety of voices and accents.

Naturally anyone paying for a course should expect to have tutors who are native speakers. Assurances that any proposed non-native speaker really does speak the language well should be ignored. If native speakers are not provided on any paid course being considered, then an alternative course should be found where native speakers will be the teachers.

To find courses and tutors:

** Look for advertisements in local and national press

** Enquire at local schools and colleges, and university further education departments

** Enquire at the public library

Attending any private course or tutorials will involve a degree of expense and it may be preferable to have the study of the language well under way at home first. It should hardly be necessary to pay a tutor to explain elementary points that could have been learned just as satisfactorily from any standard book on the target language. The available funds, if they are limited, will be better spent later, when assistance is needed with difficult points and when more will be gained from practicing what has been learned already.

8.6 Whether to have a study-friend.

Anyone working mostly on his own may begin to feel isolated and that can affect the motivation to keep going. One way to prevent this is to have a study friend or friends who are studying the same language and with whom regular sessions can be shared, studying, practicing, and exchanging tips and ideas together. Study friends can provide encouragement and prompt a greater interest in the learning of the language. Also books, audio materials and DVDs can be shared and exchanged; and there would be the possibility of clubbing together for joint private tuition.

8.7 How to learn essential grammar easily.

The importance of grammar has been discussed previously. It is not something that can sensibly be ignored if the target language is to be learned properly, and within a reasonable time-scale. And those who may be hesitant about learning grammar can be assured that approached in the right way, it can be learned comfortably, and need not be regarded, as it is so often, but mistakenly, as a boring irrelevance.

First:

Methods for understanding the grammar

** At each stage it is valuable to have some experience of the language in which the relevant point of grammar will be practiced, before any detailed study of the grammar is made. For example, skim reading the grammar explanation in a lesson to start with, so as to gain an overview, but making the first detailed study the related examples and exercises that are provided. With these clearly in mind the grammar can be studied more closely and time taken to see how and why the exercises and foreign language texts were constructed as they were.

** Reading explanations of each point of grammar in at least two different textbooks. The different approaches in each book together with different explanations will make the matter covered more easily understood and remembered.

** Using the textbooks also as grammar reference books. A note can be prepared of where the relevant grammar points, or difficult subjects, are located and a return made to them to check or confirm a construction in the language whenever necessary. Frequent referral to the different points will make them more easily remembered.

** Making written notes as the grammar is studied.

** If a great number of rules coupled with many exceptions are required for just one matter it may be easier to learn by heart a number of examples of the point in practical usage, than to try to learn a complex set of rules which in practice cannot be applied conveniently.

Second:

Methods for remembering and applying the grammar

** Writing out plenty of examples and exercises from textbooks and adding to them whenever an important new construction is encountered.

** Trying not to avoid a sentence or construction because of a perceived difficulty with the grammar but making the effort to use it.

** When referring back to a point of grammar in a textbook taking a few moments to try to memorize it.

** Discussing the grammar with a study friend.

** Practicing, practicing and practicing.

CHAPTER 9.
PROGRESSING FURTHER WITH THE FOREIGN LANGUAGE.

9.1 Is it possible for an adult to learn to speak a foreign language the way a child learns to speak?

Exactly how a child learns to speak its first language is open to some debate. It seems clear though that; first, there is a good deal of unconscious absorption by the child of phrases and expressions which are just imitated frequently and thereby learned; and secondly, that a child passes through a phase when it is particularly receptive to the learning of language.

A child has a powerful incentive to learn. It has to be able to speak the language before it can communicate adequately with anyone. It will be spoken to regularly in its native language and will be prompted and corrected as to the right form of speech. A child will not be deterred by the prospect of making mistakes; and has no thought of giving up because of difficulties, or because progress is slow. A child has no conception of such possibilities.

Also assuming that the child has perhaps 12 waking hours per day, then each week there may be up to 84 hours with significant exposure to the language. Despite all this the average child takes several years to learn the mother tongue, even to a modest standard, and will probably still be learning a more advanced vocabulary for many years after that.

Looked at in this way it will be seen that the idea of simple childlike learning of a further language is not realistic for the great majority of people. Not many would have sufficient time to do it, and such complete and constant exposure to the target language would not be achievable, without going to live in a country where only the language would be spoken. Even then the results would not be likely to be satisfactory unless some structured learning were engaged in.

However methods and suggestions can be drawn from the child's way of learning:

** Frequent listening, repeating and reciting in the target language

** Learning short phrases and sentences and putting them to use as frequently as possible.

** Not thinking about giving up.

** Making sure that mistakes are corrected. Always asking native speakers to correct any mistakes that may be made.

** Developing an understanding and use of grammar also by analogous application; although not relying just on this method.

** Being willing to get on and to start to use whatever has been learned of the language however little that may be.

Nevertheless to learn a language within a reasonable time scale something more is required:

** A realistic study plan that is followed effectively with discipline and concentration.

** An understanding of the grammar and structure of the language: of how and why words and sentences change depending upon the circumstances in which they are used &c.

** Active attempts to memorize.

** A willingness to learn a mature vocabulary rather than just a child's limited vocabulary.

A study of grammar in particular provides a most important shortcut to learning a language. Instead of having to learn variations to word usage by lengthy experience, guesswork, intuition, by being corrected, and by relying on a memory bank formed only by experience, as a child does, an adult can read up the grammar and develop it with specific examples and usage, and so progress more quickly to fluency.

95

9.2 How to find time for additional practice.

To provide additional practice during the day even small amounts of time that would otherwise be wasted can be used.

For example:

** Listening to audio materials when travelling to or from work.

** When waiting in a queue, reading over pocket note-books or flash cards.

** When out for a walk, trying to repeat from memory some of the texts or grammar that have been studied.

** Tuning the car radio to a program or playing a CD in the target language.

** Listening to audio materials on a portable player when doing routine jobs around the house.

** Taking study materials on a business trip, so as to take advantage of unoccupied moments.

9.3 How to acquire greater fluency.

Anyone who lives in a country where only the target language is spoken, and who studies it diligently and has the opportunity to speak it constantly, would more easily acquire a high degree of fluency. As this solution is unlikely to be practical except for a very few, other ways need to be found to build up fluency.

Suggestions:

** Not missing any occasion to try and speak the language especially with native speakers

** Taking holidays in or regularly visiting the country where the language is spoken and ideally staying with a family who do not speak any other language.

** Always practicing with study materials until responses, especially when translating from English to the target language, can be made without hesitation.

** Listening to radio broadcasts and watching DVDs in the language

** With audio using the pause control after each speaker and making a reply, either invented or from your memory of the recording.

** Practicing every day.

9.4 How to overcome apparent difficulties.

Inevitably when learning a foreign language apparent difficulties will be encountered from time to time. "Apparent" because usually what seems to be a difficulty will generally dissolve away to nothing with time, patience and determination as to the matter.

It should be borne in mind, when facing something that is found to be difficult, first, that if children and others can learn the language as they obviously do, then so can anyone else including you; and secondly that no one is unique in encountering difficulties. Every student of every foreign language will have had similar feelings of being unable to make progress at various stages in learning the language.

Strategies for difficulties:

** Reading another textbook covering the same point. This is always a helpful way of gaining a better understanding of studied material.

** Not avoiding learning difficult matters but equally do not letting them become stumbling blocks. Being prepared to move ahead with the study in other areas where some item may assist with an alternative view of the difficulties.

** If really feeling stuck or unable to move ahead for the moment, then moving sideways. That is, continuing to expand vocabulary, and making greater use of other learning materials that are at the same level reached. The wider knowledge acquired will provide a better basis for dealing with the difficulty when it is returned to presently.

** Expecting to encounter periods when progress seems poor. Everyone who learns a foreign language will experience difficult periods; and no-one should be deterred by when they occur. By working on steadily, it will presently be realized that there has been a real improvement.

9.5 How to deal with challenging foreign language texts.

Some foreign constructions may be more demanding than others to unravel into English. Grammar, word order, tense or mood may sometimes seem to be unduly complex compared with previous and early experience of the language.

Here are some ideas for dealing with this situation: -

** Reading the text several times taking plenty of time to think about it.

** Writing out the foreign version and trying to make a literal parallel English translation. Looking up each word in the dictionary even if previously known. There may be secondary meanings that were not immediately obvious. Double-checking tenses and moods of verbs.

** Taking a break, having a cup of tea and a walk around the block. When returning to the work refreshed, the problem will generally be found easier to deal with.

** Sleeping on it. If the text is left on one side for a day or two before it is picked up again, it will often it will be discovered that the difficulty has been solved itself in the mind, by some unconscious process, without the need for active thought about it.

** Asking others for help, but only after trying to work out the matter alone because making the effort to do so will strengthen both understanding and memory.

9.6 Use of formal and informal modes of address in the foreign language.

In every language there are different degrees of formality available for addressing someone, even if only in avoiding the use of a first name and using an appropriate title: e.g. Mr. Mrs. Miss etc. Additionally in some languages a greater formality may be commonplace, such as addressing someone in the third person. This has been more or less abandoned in English except for Royalty ... "Your Majesty"... and judges... "Your Honour" &c.

The informal as well as the formal methods of address should be learned. Otherwise, if just the formal style is relied on, you would be at a loss when the other is encountered. Generally it is best only to use the formal mode of address if it is in general use in the language, unless the informal has expressly been used to address you. Failure to do so might cause some unintentional offence, whereas greater formal politeness than necessary would never be taken amiss.

9.7 The best sources of foreign vocabulary.

The vocabulary to learn in the study of a foreign language should be that which is most in use, and of which the meaning is quite clear, preferably from having been seen or heard in context. Dictionaries are not a good source of vocabulary for learning. The volume of words is overwhelming and it is easy to be misled as to whether a word is appropriate if it has not been experienced it in actual usage.

Furthermore it is best not to trouble to learn scientific or technical words unless they are really needed.

The following will provide plentiful sources of vocabulary in the early stages of learning:

** Audio courses, textbooks and phrase books

** Children's books and beginners readers (but not comics)

** Conversations with native speakers

** Magazines and newspapers

9.8 Beware of "false friends" in foreign language vocabulary.

False friends in the context of foreign language learning, are words that appear familiar but which do not actually mean what their spelling or sound suggests. English has common roots with and influences from several other languages. Consequently some words may seem to be the same or similar to words in English, but over time they may have developed a different meaning.

If it is assumed that a foreign word means what a similar English word would mean, a mistake may be made. To avoid this difficulty vocabulary to be learned best is best taken from words in context; that is in, or taken from, phrases or sentences that support it's meaning. Moreover, unless the meaning is perfectly clear, it is safer to double-check the word with a dictionary.

9.9 Good sources of additional reading material for improving your foreign language skills.

As advances are made in the study of the target language other outlets for improving upon what has been learnt will be sought. One excellent method is to read more widely.

Suggestions:

** Beginner's readers (I.E. books with simplified texts for beginners)

** Children's books

** Magazines and Newspapers

** Collections of short stories

** Novels

Reading materials that make enjoyable reading and those that are lively and pleasant are the ones to be looked for. Anything that is too demanding or which has complex or heavily periodic sentences is best avoided. And whatever is selected should not be continued with for the time being, if it is found not to be reasonably understandable.

Constantly looking up words in the dictionary whilst reading, is very time consuming and does not make good use of the available time. And the meaning of some of the words that have already been checked so laboriously, may even be forgotten, and have to be checked again when next encountered. Moreover after a few pages of frequent word checking, it is easy to lose the thread of what was being read, and also to be disheartened by such heavy and unpleasant work.

For these reasons the advice sometimes heard "to learn a foreign language you should take a book in the language and keep on looking up every word you do not know, until you come to the end", is nonsense and should not be followed. It is best only to read a book in the language if good progress can be made without frequent use of a dictionary. Comics also are not usually good for learning. They usually contain a good deal of slang, odd usage, and children's expressions that are unlikely to be useful.

Children's books and popular novels in English that have been translated into the target language are very well worth trying, especially those which have previously been read in English, because that will make it be easier to follow the foreign version. Both the English and the foreign versions should be bought and each compared with the other, the relevant pages in both being open at the same time. Also the English edition could be referred to (instead of a dictionary) if some part of the foreign version is not understood. A further good exercise is to read the foreign text and then to try translating passages from the English version into the foreign, and then to check the attempt against the foreign version.

Being able to read foreign books of literary worth and also poetry in the target language is a wonderful experience and one of the great pleasures that will come with learning a foreign language. All the same, for the reasons given, it is better to wait until sufficient facility has been gained with the language so that it can be read flowingly and without frequent stops for word checks.

9.10 Some quick tips for easy learning.

** Putting labels on objects around the house with the foreign word for them and saying the foreign word whenever the object is used.

** Keeping a progress chart and marking progress as each lesson is completed.

** Using the foreign language to write out shopping lists and personal notes.

** Keeping a diary in the foreign language.

** If a mistake is made, reciting the correct version aloud ten times.

** Finding a recipe book in the foreign language and at least once a week cooking a meal using a recipe from it, and whilst doing so describing aloud in the language each step taken.

CHAPTER 10.
ADVANCED FOREIGN LANGUAGE LEARNING TECHNIQUES. AND AIDS.

10.1 How to become fluent with numbers in the foreign language.

The way to overcome any difficulty with numbers is with plentiful practice.

Suggestions:

** When checking the time saying it aloud in the foreign language

** When a mileage sign is passed saying it aloud in the foreign language

** When shopping checking the prices of the goods purchased and saying them in the foreign language

** When using a calculator saying the figures in the foreign language as they are tapped in, and then saying the final total.

** When writing in the foreign language always writing out all the numbers as words, not as figures.

10.2 Tips for remembering vocabulary gender.

English pays almost no attention to the gender of a noun. How tiresome it is then that many other languages make a distinction between masculine and feminine and even neuter, with different word variations for nouns, adjectives, articles etc. depending upon gender. Tiresome or not, if there are gender differences in the language they will have to learned.

The following will help:

** Always learning the article with the noun.

For example:

In English the articles are: the, a, an.

In Spanish: el, la, un, una.

In French: le, la, un, une.

** When a word is learned, visualizing it with a strong memory link in a masculine or feminine context as appropriate.

** Where practical, learning the gender with the word in a sentence or phrase.

** If an error is made, repeating the correct gender article and the noun aloud ten times to help reinforce it on the memory.

10.3 Making your own foreign language audio recordings.

Audio is an invaluable foreign language tool, so that it is worth considering home-made recordings if they are not obtainable by other means. Obviously this should be done with native speakers. It is not worth bothering to record those who do not have the language as their mother tongue and nor should the student's own voice be recorded, because of the risk of perpetuating any pronunciation errors when working with the recording. It is important to have the tones and accents of native speakers to listen to, so that they can be imitated with confidence.

Luckily there are audio course available in a great number of languages, so it generally should be possible to find something to suit beginners and probably those who are more advanced as well. All the same it may be advantageous to have some home made audio, especially if the language is not otherwise well covered.

Careful thought should be given to what is to be recorded. Passages and exercises from course books, from readers and from phrase books could be part of the selection. Also it is best not to rely on just one speaker.

Ideally the help of several should be enlisted so as to provide experience with different voices.

When learning to cope with fast speech, having a tailor-made recording can be particularly helpful. The speaker could be asked to record at conversation speed; or radio or TV conversations or bulletins could be recorded and then the speaker asked to write down exactly what was said and perhaps to record it again in his own voice a little more slowly. Listening to both these recordings and repeating them out loud will provide very satisfactory practice.

10.4 The principle of over-learning for foreign languages and how to apply it.

Over-learning in the context of language learning, requires that, when each portion of a course is studied, it is better to continue for a little while after the matters covered have been grasped and until a really easy recall of what has been learned is achieved. For example: when memorizing vocabulary, continuing until it can be recited quite fluently, whether what has been memorized are single words or complete phrases.

Likewise when translating, not being satisfied with a translation that has been just plodded through even though it has been done accurately. Instead going over it several times until it can be rattled of quickly, speaking aloud, and switching from the target language to the English and back again without faltering

Over-learning will impose the material more deeply and effectively on the memory and reduce the risk of it fading subsequently.

10.5 How to learn to think in the foreign language.

A critical watershed in the learning of a foreign language is the moment at which it is found to be possible for the first time to think in the foreign language. When this occurs the study will become easier and more rewarding. No longer is it necessary first to decide in English what is to be said and then to translate into the foreign language before speaking. The thinking and the foreign speech can both be the same. With this advantage new vocabulary falls more easily into place and so is more readily learned; and likewise grammatical structures are absorbed with less need for analysis and deliberate memorization. .

Many of the methods described elsewhere in this book will be recognized in the following suggestions for encouraging thinking in the target language: -

** Where practical, using the foreign word order in English study translations. This will prompt thinking in the foreign word order.

** Regularly using practice sessions in audio in which questions are asked and to which answers have to be made up; preferably with little time to think before the response has to be given.

** Speaking frequently in the foreign language however badly. If there is no-one else to talk to, then talking to oneself in the language.

** Writing letters and essays in the target language.

** Repeating audio lessons regularly so that the words and word patterns sink into the subconscious. Likewise, keeping on working away at words, sentences and phrases until they are known really well (over-learned) so that the they become a reflex and it is no longer necessary to think about what they mean. In this way they will come back to mind and will be used spontaneously without the need to translate from English.

** Listening to radio television and films in the foreign language. When listening to these there is often little time to translate and thinking in the language is the easier option.

** Memorizing texts in the target language. See further below as to this.

10.6 Use this little-known but very effective technique to achieve a substantial boost to your command of the foreign language.

A little known but very valuable aid to learning a foreign language, is the memorization of texts in the target language. As discussed previously, this was one of the methods employed with success by Charlotte Bronte. All that has to be done is to select suitable texts and then to give time to committing them to memory. A target of say two or at most three pages a week to be memorized would be ideal for the purpose. The improvement that this exercise can provide in the command of the language is considerable.

The practice of memorization is not now in fashion, but in the days before radio and television, it was commonplace for poetry, selections from literary works, and famous speeches, for example from Shakespeare, to be memorized, so that recitals could be given for private enjoyment. Nothing extraordinary was thought of the practice; which, even as it was not then unusual, was not found to be an unduly hard task either.

Nowadays not even schoolchildren are given lines to learn, and it seems that it is only actors and singers who memorize by heart; but their evident success in doing so, even with very lengthy parts, is proof that memorizing is not particularly difficult once the habit is acquired. This should serve as encouragement for those who may feel that memorizing like this would not be possible for them.

For language learning there is no need to memorize anything particularly lengthy. The idea is just to memorize suitable passages extracted for the purpose. Something short could be attempted as a trial. It will be discovered that it is not in fact a very hard task to memorize, and with each subsequent text confidence grows and the task becomes easier.

The reason that memorizing foreign language texts is so advantageous, is that it gives a significant boost to fluency by helping to build up a fund, a memory bank, of expressions and phrases that can be drawn on and adapted when speaking. It will also improve confidence in using the language. Lastly, and most importantly, it will encourage and assist you greatly to begin to stop thinking in English and then translating into the target language, and instead to begin to think in the target language. This of course is an essential step towards achieving fluency.

It is not of course necessary to be word perfect as an actor would be. It is sufficient to be able to recite in the target language the gist of the text, perhaps with an occasional peek at the text for a prompt as to the beginning of a line. Nor is it needful to be able to remember the selected text for any great period of time. It is enough that it can be recalled during the week or so following the memorization. After that, whether remembered fully or not, it will be in the subconscious and working to aid and influence the use of the target language.

In many ways learning a text by heart is easier than memorizing individual and unconnected phrases and sentences, because of the narrative that a text provides, and the cohesion that this gives to the words in the memory. Numerous words can be remembered when they are all held together by the narrative, or theme that the text covers. Recollection of a portion of a memorized text brings back other related portions; and when a particular word or phrase is wanted for some other purpose, in conversation for example, it will be more readily brought back to mind by recollection of the subject matter in the text.

One method of memorizing a text that may be found to be helpful is as follows.

1. Having selected the text to be memorized, highlight either the first word or two at the beginning of each sentence, or a key word somewhere in the sentence. Break down any sentences that are unduly long, into shorter clauses, and amalgamate any sentences that are too short.

2. Taking each sentence in turn, continue to read it aloud several times (repetition), until you find you can speak it without looking at the text, and then do so several times more (recitation).

3. When the whole text has been completed in this way, return to the beginning and using just the highlighted words as a prompt, try to recite the rest of each sentence or clause. In the event of any failure, then repeat 2 above for that sentence.

4. The highlighted words at the beginning of each sentence could be written down on a separate slip of paper, so that the remainder of the sentence cannot be seen when they are used as a prompt.

5. If memorizing a text for which you have an audio recording, which incidentally is highly recommended, make a point also of listening regularly to the recording, and of reciting each sentence after it has been heard. This is an aid to memorization and in addition your pronunciation will in this way be kept accurate.

6. When memorizing a text do not keep returning right back to the beginning when you make a mistake or if you have to recheck the text for accuracy. If you do so, you will just become more proficient in reciting the earlier parts of the text than the final parts, which will not have been gone over so often.

7. It is sufficient to be able to recite each sentence using the prompt. It is not necessary to be able to recite the text without doing so, because the

prompt does not diminish the benefit of the memorization as an aid to learning the target language.

Suitable passages for memorization by heart are those that include everyday situations and typical conversations. They do not have to be taken from language course materials, although these will be excellent to start with. An alternative would be passages from children's books, with some adventure and excitement. Such books can offer a surprising amount of text covering excellent ground for memorization in the target language: e.g. food, travel, family situations, getting into scrapes, dealing with awkward situations, meeting people, &c. Especially valuable are texts and especially course materials for which you have an audio recording because as indicated above, the audio is an additional aid to memorizing and will assist you in ensuring that your accent does not stray away from correct pronunciation.

10.7 Why offensive language should never be used.

However amusing it may seem at the time, it is always a mistake to use offensive language, diminishing the speaker rather than raising him in the estimation of others and likely to exclude him from their company in future. This is true about such usage in English and even more so in a foreign language where offence may easily be caused, especially as cultural boundaries may not be what they have been assumed to be; and where the result of causing offence may be more serious than might have been imagined.

10.8 Finding opportunities to speak the foreign language.

Writing and reading in the target language are essential skills, but before anyone can properly say that they speak the language, they need to be able to do just that with some fluency. To achieve this it is important to take every opportunity to talk with native speakers and not to be held back by reasons such as shyness or lack of a complete command of the language.

And there is nothing quite so likely to give impetus to the study of the target language, as the pleasure that will be gained from actually communicating in the language with someone for whom it is their mother tongue, and appreciating that the efforts to learn the language are really bearing fruit.

So whenever native speakers of the target language are encountered an effort should be made to exchange at least a few words with them. What has been learned so far can be employed, even though it may be little more than a handful of polite expressions and phrases. Once this has been tried a few times it will be discovered that most people respond pleasantly and politely to a friendly approach and to attempts to speak their language.

Preparation for these opportunities can be made by rehearsing the sort of small talk that most people engage in when they meet a stranger. For example by practicing with appropriate phrases and sentences to supply a suitable fund to draw on when a conversation is started; and to give a better chance of understanding the reply.

Opportunities for meeting native speakers may arise through introductions or academic and business contacts etc. Or they may be encountered casually, perhaps as tourists in a shop or cafe, and by hearing them speak in the target language. The chance has then to be taken and a polite enquiry made as to whether they are French, or Spanish, or German etc. and then some friendly remark made. And then continue with a conversation about-----holidays-----or travel----or employment----or family------any topic will do as long as the effort is made.

When a country where the target language is spoken, is visited there will be numerous opportunities of speaking it that need to be grasped and not allowed to slip past. For example those who are travelling should avoid using a hire-car, as inevitably opportunities to meet and speak to people will be fewer. When a bus or train is taken, there will be the chance to sit next to someone and open a conversation with him or her.

Similar opportunities can be looked for in cafes, bars and at the hotel. Shop assistants can be asked to help with some purchases, to explain the way to the next place to be visited, or perhaps to recommend places in the town that are worth seeing. Perhaps it will be possible at the same time for other subjects to be touched on as well.

10.9 How to cope with fast speech in the foreign language.

An opportunity has arisen of speaking the language with a native speaker and what has been learned so far has been tried out, using appropriate phrases and expressions. The person responds with a burst of speech that is not fully understood. This problem is not unusual because in normal speech in any language, the words are only rarely expressed as clear-cut individual words, but are likely to be run together.

How should with this situation be dealt with?

** By expecting it to happen so that when it does, it will not be off-putting.

** By remembering that it is not necessary to understand every part of what is said. This is especially the case with polite exchanges. Sometimes it may be easier and more expedient for a nod and smile to be given and another sentence attempted.

** By explaining that the language is only spoken a little and asking the person to speak more slowly and to repeat what was just said.

** By trying to bring the conversation round to subjects, perhaps of lesser importance, that can be understood and talked about more easily.

** By training the ear by listening to the radio or to recordings of fast speech whilst following with a transcript of the target language.

** By not ever giving up. By keeping going, attempting to understand and making an effort to reply, and realizing that improvements will come as confidence grows.

10.10 Inaccuracies in foreign language conversation.

During any conversation with a native speaker of the target language it is inevitable that those who are learning will make mistakes. This should not be a cause for concern. If the language is going to be learned the effort must be made to speak it, even when only just starting to learn. It really does not matter that mistakes are made sometimes or even often. The value of the experience to be gained by engaging in spontaneous live speech is infinitely more important.

Moreover as long as the main idea is put over, a few errors are unlikely to be significant. The sense of what is intended can often be conveyed with just a part of the sentence. As for what is not understood, the other person will try and guess or probably give a prompt, just as an English speaker would if the roles were reversed.

CHAPTER 11.

AIMING AT COMPLETE MASTERY OF THE FOREIGN. LANGUAGE.

11.1 How to use interest in the culture as an aid for foreign language learning.

An interest in the culture, the activities and the news of countries where the target language is spoken will sharpen the appetite for learning the language as well.

Suggestions: -

** Learning about the history

** Following the politics and the sport

** Reading newspapers and magazines in the language

** Joining a society associated with the language

** Reading literature and poetry in the language

** Listening to radio broadcasts in the language.

** Watching films from the countries where the language is spoken.

11.2 How to assist your progress with greater enjoyment from the study and use of the foreign language.

The more study of the language can be enjoyed and what has been learned put to use, the more incentive there will be to learn and maintain the progress being made.

Suggestions: -

** Watching films and DVDs in the language.

** Joining a society connected with the language and take part in the activities.

** Making friends with native speakers.

** Reading often and widely in the language.

** As progress is made, advancing to more challenging novels and literary works.

** Subscribing to a magazine in the language that covers some special interest or hobby in which you have an interest.

** Taking a holiday in the country where the language is spoken.

11.3 Learning verbs and their conjugations. How to make the task easier.

Learning the verbs for a foreign language with their various conjugations and especially with any exceptions to the rules, that may generally apply to them, can be one of the more demanding tasks in the learning of a foreign language.

Here are some tips to make the process easier.

** When beginning to learn the target language, it is likely that just one tense at a time will be studied. But it is important as soon as possible to have an understanding of all the tenses. So at an early stage an attempt should be made to gain an overview of all the verb types, formations, tenses and conjugations in the language. The usual method for undertaking an overview should be followed, and then a chart made of the various verb structures for future reference.

Now each of the verb types turn can be learned, but without trying to become word perfect before moving on to the next. A return to each with more practice can be made in the future, ideally many times.

** Patterns and relationships in the verb formations that may not be evident when studying just one tense at a time should be looked for. When some knowledge of all the tenses for a particular verb has been acquired, patterns may start to be seen both for that verb and for other verbs, and they are a helpful aid to learning and remembering.

** As soon as practical, a target should be set of studying a single new verb, conjugated in all its tenses, every day. There are many excellent reference books for different languages, providing collections of verbs each fully conjugated in all tenses, typically with a whole page devoted to each verb. With the benefit of such a book just one verb can be taken every day and studied for a few minutes. In this way it should be possible to ensure good progress in the understanding and command of the different verbs forms.

The verbs that are the most essential, or commonly used, should be concentrated on to start with. It is helpful also to chant aloud the conjugations of the daily verb whilst it is read, in the same way that multiplication tables are learned. By reading over the conjugations and reciting in this way an intuitive feel for the verbs in the target language will soon begin to develop, aided of course by the benefits of analogous application.

** The regular forms of verb conjugations for each verb type need to be memorized. But there is no need to try and memorize all of the conjugated forms for every individual verb that you chance to come across. Provided that you stick to studying fully a one new verb a day as described above, it will be found with time that the way to conjugate the others will be acquired naturally. With irregular verb forms however, some effort to memorize will have to be made, but with the routine of one verb per day still being stuck to.

** A point should be made of learning some key verbs or phrases that will assist in overcoming any limitations in verb knowledge or when the memory fails in conversation. For example, ways in which the infinitive form can be used might be learned, coupled with a phrase that is known well. Suppose that the expression "Help me" is needed. This is an imperative verb form but suppose that the correct mood and tense in the target language is not known or cannot be remembered. Perhaps instead "Can you help me?" or "I need help" could be said. Similar useful auxiliary expressions are "I want-----"---"Would you like-----"----"I have-----"----"Do you know how to-----".

Compound verb forms based on commonly used verbs and past or present participles are also important to learn due to the wide range of expressions that they can open up. And in many of the European languages for example, the compound tenses are easier to learn than the others.

11.4 Some easily available additional learning resources for foreign language learning.

** FILMS AND DVDs.

Foreign language films are an excellent way of gaining further experience with the target language, although ideally they should have subtitles that can be ignored later as proficiency increases. DVDs are better than a film at the cinema; the pause, rewind, and replay controls on the player can be used to hear again any dialogue that was missed or found difficult.

Also with a DVD a decision can be made to have the subtitles on or off, and even whether to have them in English or in the foreign language. Both are valuable although it may be best to begin with, to have foreign language subtitles so as to follow the exact words when they are reflected in the subtitle. Regrettably this may not always be possible, and unfortunately subtitles are sometimes just a summary of what has been said with portions of the spoken dialogue left out altogether.

Nonetheless the benefit that can be gained from foreign language DVDs is substantial; and they also provide the pleasure of relaxing with a film whilst thinking, not untruthfully, that there has been no shirking from the important work of learning the target language.

The best films are those made in the target language. Those originally made in English and dubbed are not quite so satisfactory for studying the language, because the dubbing can be a distraction and there will be something missing from the foreign feel of the film.

** TELEVISION

Television in the target language may be available on cable or satellite and whilst they are unlikely to have the benefit of English subtitles, it will give plentiful exposure to both speech and culture in the language. With some programs especially such as news or comedies it will be possible to deduce the meaning of what is said from the scenes.

** RADIO.

Radio like television will greatly assist the ear to follow the sound of the target language. But unlike TV, which may not be so readily available in the language, it should be easy to find a radio program somewhere in the target language, if only on shortwave.

** THE INTERNET.

This internet provides innumerable foreign language resources: culture, information, details about the countries where the target language is spoken, and text written in the language. A few words typed into one of the search engines will bring plentiful useful material.

** NEWSPAPERS AND MAGAZINES.

Many foreign language publications are available at major newsagents, so there is a good chance of finding one in the target language. Alternatively it may be possible to obtain one by subscription. Magazines covering not very demanding subjects, perhaps with plenty of pictures that tell part of the story, will be best to begin with.

With media resources the object is to add entertainment and fun to the study and not to make the media the study itself. Anything that proves to be difficult to follow should be left on one side until the language skills improve to the necessary standard for it to be enjoyed.

11.5 Use this alternative dictionary to develop deeper learning of the foreign language.

The first foreign language dictionary to be purchased would naturally be the usual bilingual form with both foreign language and English provided. A valuable addition is a monolingual dictionary with just the foreign language and with definitions given only in that language. Whilst a bilingual dictionary will always be needed, if only to look up the foreign translation of English words, there are many advantages in having a monolingual dictionary as well.

A monolingual dictionary: -

** Develops comprehension and learning of foreign words in the foreign language itself.

** Gives a better understanding of the real meaning of the foreign word than would be possible when merely reading about it in English.

** Reduces dependence on English in understanding the foreign language

** Aids memorization of the words checked because they will have been learned in context and without reliance on English.

** Encourages thinking in the foreign language.

11.6 How to improve self-confidence as an aid to learning the foreign language.

Feeling confident is a tonic that will encourage anyone to do better and progress faster, and there are various ways in which confidence in the language study can be improved.

Suggestions: -

** Remembering, when a difficult area is encountered, that many others have learned the language and that you can do so just as well as they have.

** Practicing speaking with native speakers frequently as recommended. Even if conversations are very limited, it will give a real boost to be able to undertake active speech in the language.

** Bearing in mind that whether one learns faster or slower than others is unimportant. What matters, is that progress is made by undertaking some study, every day, towards completion of the key plan. If this is done success will certainly follow.

** Utilizing some of the ideas suggested for gaining greater enjoyment from the study of the foreign language. Pleasure taken in the language will increase self-confidence and vice versa. A virtuous circle will be created.

** Undertaking regular self-assessments and charting the progress made. The assessment will provide proof that the target language skills are improving.

** Saying to yourself every day "my ability with-----target language-----is getting better and better-----I am making good progress". This is an application of the theory of Coueism to foreign language learning.

11.7 The importance of rewards.

The key plan sets out the stages to be achieved in the language study and the conclusion of each stage is the next target to be aimed at. It's always a good idea to take a little reward when doing well. Doing so when the target is reached provides a useful further incentive to study, so that a bit more push is given towards completion of the task and the eventual success.

For example a night out or a meal at a restaurant might be taken as each stage in the key plan is completed; and a foreign holiday would be an obvious reward when the key plan for the course of study is completed. More minor stages can be marked with less substantial rewards. The self-reward system can even be adopted on a daily basis. Some small treat could enjoyed when the days allotted study is finished; but of course denied when there has been a failure to complete the work.

11.8 How to cope with (and prevent) flagging interest in the foreign language study.

In any study a point may come when the initial keenness wears thin. This is a common experience and there are several strategies for dealing with it.

Suggestions: -

** Rereading the motivation list.

** Setting a fresh and better reward to be taken when the next stage is reached.

** Doing a self-assessment and seeing the real progress that has been made so far.

** Finding a native speaker and practicing conversation. This will be very good for self-confidence, and will help rekindle enthusiasm.

** Taking a short break in the country where the language is spoken.

** Fresh air, exercise and adequate sleep are all good ways to be revitalized. After taking plenty and feeling refreshed, the study can be returned to with renewed determination.

11.9 Why and how regular self-assessments of progress in the foreign language should be made.

Those who contemplate the amount of work ahead may overlook what has been gained already and allow themselves, without good reason, to become disheartened with the study. The object of the self-assessment is to prevent this occurring, and to encourage confidence in the progress of the study. The assessment does this by drawing attention to how far the study has progressed, and what has been achieved, rather than dwelling on how far there is to go.

Suggestions for regular self-assessments: -

** Checking the key plan and making a note of how well the study discipline has been kept up and of what has been learned so far.

** Checking how well a new text in the target language, not previously worked on, can be understood.

** Listening to the television or radio and noting how many words are recognized in a fixed period: say 3 minutes.

** Writing down the results of the self-assessment, comparing it with the last such assessment and keeping it for future reference.

11.10 Learning the target language in the language itself

When a reasonable command of the language has been achieved, it is of considerable advantage to the further development of the skills, to begin to study the language simply in the language itself. This means abandoning the use of English and the props that go with it such as English translations, a bilingual dictionary and textbooks in English; saying goodbye to the parallel method; and relying in future just upon learning based on reading and writing, hearing and speaking the target language.

Naturally the prospect of having no further help from English based resources may not seem very appealing at first sight, but subject to the proviso that some fair ability should have first been acquired with the target language, learning just through the medium of the language, should not be unduly difficult. Moreover this is an important way in which real fluency in the language can be realized.

Suggestions for learning in the target language itself: -

If possible acquire and study a textbook in the language for use by foreigners. For example in some languages there are books available along the lines of "Target Language for foreigners".

Read widely in the language.

Listen to the language spoken without having any English prompts.

Use audio without any transcript.

Use a monolingual dictionary (discussed above).

Watch films in the language with no English subtitles and presently without any subtitles at all.

Have conversations in the language as often as possible and preferably with those who do not speak any English.

When a difficulty is encountered, seek help only from sources in the language itself.

Memorize passages from texts in the language.

Listen to radio programs in the language.

Regularly write in the language.

Many of the above suggestions reflect ideas and methods discussed previously; the difference here is that there must be a fixed resolution in future to approach and learn the target language only by using the language itself.

CHAPTER 12.

MAKING SURE OF YOUR SUCCESS WITH THE CHOSEN FOREIGN LANGUAGE.

12.1 How to revise the foreign language effectively.

Just as important as regular study of the target language is regular revision of what has been learned to date. Regular revision is necessary to make sure that everything has been properly understood and remembered; that it is impressed more deeply on the memory; and that it is not allowed to fade.

Revision program suggestions: -

** A first revision, of any days study, should always be carried out at the end of the day.

** A second revision of the same work should be carried out after several days have passed.

** A third revision should be carried out after a month or so.

** A further revision is desirable after the expiration of several months.

12.2 Alternative foreign language revision methods.

A natural inclination on completing the whole or a portion of a course, is to revise the work by starting again at the beginning and following through to the point reached, before then carrying on from there. The downside to revising like this is that it may easily result in a better knowledge of the earlier parts of the course than the later parts that are almost invariably the more demanding. This will especially be the case if the later stages of the study have been skimped, perhaps due to a desire to reach the end more quickly.

Suggestions: -

** Not always going back to the beginning when revising. Instead devising a rolling revision program, so that for each new lesson undertaken, just one from an earlier part of the course is revised, each time moving the revised lesson forward. For example, after reaching lesson 10 say, lesson 1 is then revised before progressing to lesson 11; then lesson 2 is revised before going on to study lesson 12, and so on.

** On subsequent revisions two lessons might be revised for each new lesson, so that the revision slowly catches up with the main study.

** Revising sometimes by working backwards from the last lesson studied towards the first. The later lessons, being more advanced, are probably more essential for revision than the simpler subject matter or the early ones; and as progress is made backwards the work should become easier.

** Paying more attention to revising the later and more difficult lessons in the course, than the earlier ones.

12.3 The lazy man's way to learn a foreign language.

The method almost invariably used by lazy learners of a foreign language is that of listening to and trying to use or to repeat, what they hear said (or, more likely, only what they think they have heard said) by speakers of the language. Also, whether consciously or otherwise, they are guided by analogous application. The lazy foreign language learner does not condescend to what he would regard as the artifice of studying, certainly does not trouble to find out about the grammar of the target language and views with distaste any suggestion that it would help him to do so. He avoids textbooks and anything that looks like formal instruction.

This is a method of learning for which, to make any progress at all, it is essential that the learner should be living in a country where the language is spoken. Indeed the favourite mantra of the lazy language-learner is the old false-claim "the only way to learn a foreign language is by going to live in the country". But, as has already been discussed, just living in a

123

country of the target language without studying it, is not a very efficient learning method or likely to yield good results despite the benefit of being regularly in the company of people who speak the language; although some people may be lucky and achieve a degree of success by lazy method.

The most probable outcome for the lazy learner is that the use of the language will be limited and ungrammatical, that the vocabulary will be poor and that many mistakes will be made. Moreover the language spoken may all too easily be just a pidgin version, stunted, ungrammatical and unattractive. These are good reasons not to adopt the lazy learner's method with the target language.

However for those who are only looking for a quick way to learn a minimum of the language or who are determined to do as little as possible and are willing to accept a low level of ability sufficient for just simple communication in the language, then the following suggestions will help to make best use of the limited time and effort that they are prepared to make available for the study.

Suggestions: -

** Using a beginners audio and play it in an MP3 as often as possible.

** Learning phrases from a phrase book.

** Concentrating on learning just the most essential 500 words in the target language. Which are the most essential? Those covered in the beginners audio and phrase book will probably be sufficient, but if need be more could be selected from standard textbooks to make up the number desired

** Using the memory link method to learn individual words and the group method for phrases.

** Learning the following verb tenses as a minimum: - the past, the past imperfect, the present, and the future. Note that many of the compound tenses (E.G. "I have arrived", "I had arrived", "I shall have arrived", "I would have arrived") in some of the European languages are relatively easy to master. These could be learned as well.

** Using flash cards on which are written out all the important points.

** Studying every day and dividing up the limited time given to learning the language so as to have two equal studying sessions per day: one in the morning and one at night. Also revising regularly. It is important not to let the limited efforts be wasted due to a failure to revise.

** Watching DVDs in the target language.

** Reading about the grammar in a course book even if no attempt is made to learn it. This way there may at least be a distant memory of the subject by way of a starting point for future reference.

** Talking with speakers of the target language whenever possible.

The lazy man's way to learn a foreign language, even when improved by the steps suggested above is not to be recommended; and it really would be regrettable not to make the effort to learn the language properly. The rewards to be enjoyed as a result of diligent learning, would amply repay the time devoted to the task that would be found increasingly to be easier and more enjoyable as progress is made.

12.4 How to avoid letting the foreign language skills fade away.

The effort has been made, the study has been completed, and the target language can be spoken. Exams have been passed, promotion gained, the desired foreign contract signed up, or the other objects achieved for which the language was learned.

It is important now not to let the benefits of the work fade away due to lack of use, as inevitably they would, just because the language is not needed at the moment. Knowledge of a foreign language and ability to speak it, has so much to give, and it should not be regarded as just an academic milestone.

Suggestions: -

** Setting a higher target of ability, and starting to study towards it with a more advanced course in the language.

** Trying occasional total immersion in the language to polish the skills still further, perhaps by taking an annual week or so at a language school in a country where it is spoken.

** Reading regularly in the language: novels, poetry, magazines etc.

** Making the language and the cultures from which it comes a lifetime hobby.

** Travelling in the countries where the language is spoken.

** Making friends with native speakers of the language.

** Enjoying films in the language.

12.5 Putting it all together and the global approach.

With the benefit of the different techniques commanded, a campaign for learning the chosen foreign language can be planned.

First: Preparation:

** Making a resolution to learn the target language coupled with a determination not to be deflected from it for any reason.

** Writing out a Motivation List.

** Researching the essential materials for learning that will be needed so as to get started, the textbooks and audio etc., and then acquiring them.

** Checking availability of native speakers.

** Deciding on a time scale for learning and working out how often and how much studying will be done.

** Preparing a Key Plan.

** Deciding how and where most of the studying is to be done: the place, the background circumstances etc.

** Researching and deciding upon a course at a college, or having private tuition,

** Finding a study friend.

** Undertaking an overview of the language study materials.

Second: Learning the language:

When starting the work it is necessary always to be prepared always to vary the approach and to bear in mind, as has already been emphasized that the learning of a foreign language should not be undertaken just from one direction or by concentrating on just one method. It is better and much more effective to employ a variety of methods.

Moreover, especially when beginning, it is important for the individual to find out what works best by trying out different approaches. The most successful techniques should be brought to bear, as convenient, on the target language that should be viewed as a global objective to be tackled from several different angles and directions. A varied approach like this will make the study more interesting and enjoyable and will be more likely to yield the desired result of fluency.

12.6 A short list of useful terms.

The following terms are amongst the most common that will be met with in the grammar sections of any standard textbook. There is no need to attempt to learn them. They are provided only so that they can be referred when necessary, and by doing so it will soon be found that they are known well enough.

** Verb: A word that indicates the action in a sentence. E.G. The horse galloped. "Galloped" is the verb.

** Tense: The form of the verb that indicates the time of the action. E.G. Present, Past, Future etc.

** Active or Passive Verb:

Active: the subject carries out the action. E.G. The horse jumped over the fence.

Passive: The subject suffers the action. E.G. The fence was cut down.

** Reflexive verb: A verb in which the action turns back upon the subject. E.G. He stopped himself. English is not too bothered about reflexive forms but in some languages the verb is frequently in a reflexive form.

** Infinitive verb: The infinitive is the verb in its purest form, unaltered in any way. In English the infinitive is recognizable because it includes the word "to". E.G. To run. To read. To sleep.

** Mood: The form of the verb that expresses the mode or manner or state of the action. E.G.- Indicative mood: the verb when it just affirms or denies something. E.G. The horse ran the race.

Imperative mood: The verb when it expresses command or advice. E.G. Come here now. Stop that.

Subjunctive mood: The verb when it expresses condition, hypotheses or contingency. E.G. If I were you. He may have arrived. He should have arrived.

In English the subjunctive is used far less frequently than in some other languages.

** Conjugate: To give the various inflections or parts of a verb (i.e. in a desired tense).

Example: the present indicative tense verb To Be in English conjugated: -

First person singular: I am,

Second person singular: You are,

Third person singular: He is,

First person plural: We are,

Second person plural: You are,

Third person plural: They are.

** Adverb: A word that describes a verb. E.G. He shouted excitedly. The cat purred happily.

** Adjective: A word that describes a noun. E.G. A broken egg. 'Broken' is the adjective.

** Article: The name given to the following words: 'the' (definitive article), 'a' & 'a (indefinite article).

** Decline: To change the words as necessary depending on different circumstances, E.G. I gave the book to him? He has the book.

** Noun: A word for a person, place, or thing. E.G. Book, Horse, etc.

** Pronoun: Any word that may be use instead of using the noun itself. E.G. The book was mine and I read it. "It" is the pronoun.

** Person: There are six possible persons, as follows.

First person singular: I

Second person singular: You (only one of you)

Third person singular: He

First person plural: We

Second person plural: You (more than one of you)

Third person plural: They

** Present participle: In English where the form of the verb ends with the letters ING it is called the present participle. E.G. He was talking; "talking" is here the present participle. Note that the participle is sometimes used as an adjective.

** Past participle: In English the verb is described as a past participle in the form in which it is added to another verb to give an indication of the past. E.G. He has spoken. He has stopped.

12.7 The important first step.

Having read this book, nothing more is wanting for you to learn your own target language, than the determination both to start and then to pursue the study diligently. It is up to you; and you can do it, you really can learn to speak a foreign language, perhaps several, and with the minimum of effort and difficulty if the methods described here are followed.

So do not be tempted to put off the day of action. Make the resolution and start planning the course of study now. A new world of interesting languages and their cultures awaits you, as well as a lifetime of pleasure in the languages learned, and numerous friends amongst the people to be met in the process.

There is a Chinese saying "the journey of a thousand miles begins with one step". Take that important first step now and then take each succeeding step, without worrying about how far there is to go after that, and the destination will then surely be reached. And even before you arrive, it will be discovered that the journey has itself become both pleasurable and immensely rewarding.

Now we have reached the end of this book and nothing remains but to wish you good luck, happiness and great enjoyment with every foreign language that you may ever decide to learn

Also by Peter Oakfield

How to transform your Memory and Brain Power: a complete course for memory development, fast learning skills and speed-reading.

Lightning Source UK Ltd.
Milton Keynes UK
UKOW031813020113

204337UK00001B/4/P